Canon Mike Chew has been the Business Excellence Director for Philips Lighting, and was responsible for the development and implementation of the Philips global improvement strategy process, while at the same time being churchwarden of an Anglican parish in Lancashire. He is currently serving as MAP and growth strategy facilitator for the Blackburn diocese.

Mark Ireland was formerly diocesan missioner for the Lichfield diocese, and is now vicar of All Saints Wellington with St Catherine's Eyton. He is a member of General Synod and co-author of *Evangelism – which way now?* (Church House Publishing, second edition, 2005) and *Evangelism in a Spiritual Age* (Church House Publishing, 2005).

HOW TO DO MISSION ACTION PLANNING

A *vision-centred approach*

Mike Chew and Mark Ireland

First published in Great Britain in 2009

Society for Promoting Christian Knowledge
36 Causton Street
London SW1P 4ST
www.spckpublishing.co.uk

British Library Cataloguing-in-Publication Data
A catalogue record for this book is available from the British Library

ISBN 978–0–281–06122–8

Typeset by Graphicraft Limited, Hong Kong
First printed in Great Britain by Ashford Colour Press
Subsequently digitally printed in Great Britain

Produced on paper from sustainable forests

Contents

Figures and Tables

Figures

Figures and Tables

Tables

Acknowledgements

We are very grateful to all those who have so willingly shared their hard-won experience and expertise – particularly to:

- Those dioceses that have contributed material to us and have been willing for it to be published on the <http://www.churchmaps.co.uk> website.
- Peter Hill, whose initial research into MAP provided materials for the churchmaps website and helped to spark the idea of producing this book.
- Roger Longworth who gave his time to become the webmaster of churchmaps.
- Bishop David Hope, for offering to write the Foreword.
- Those who have contributed ideas and suggestions during the writing process, especially Richard Adams, Damian Feeney, +Nicholas Reade, Godfrey Stone, Robert Warren and Paul Wordsworth.

Mark Ireland and Mike Chew

Foreword

One of the many and daunting tasks with which any bishop is charged at his ordination is that he should not only 'lead in serving and caring for the people of God' but that he should also 'promote' the Church's mission throughout the world.

It was therefore in the context of the primacy of mission and evangelization that in each of the dioceses in which I have been privileged to serve I have sought to take some initiative which would fulfil the charge which I had been given and thereby encourage and further that mission entrusted to us by Christ to announce the Kingdom and make disciples.

The first opportunity came when as Bishop of my place of birth – Wakefield – the diocese celebrated its centenary. Together with the then staff team we launched an initiative which encouraged each parish quite literally to produce a map – a geographical map – of its parish area and to mark on it where the church was and where church members came from and where other important gathering places – shops, clubs, schools, pubs etc. – were in relation to the church. This in itself was both educative and revealing, not least to members of the church! This 'map', we suggested, should be displayed at the entrance of every church with words of welcome, together with photographs of people and places, also that the 'map' itself be used as a basis for discussion and planning for mission as the diocese, in celebrating one hundred years, looked ahead to the next hundred!

The 'maps' which came to be produced both in London and York were of a rather different nature. Having spent a good deal of time visiting and listening in the first instance in each of the dioceses, I concluded that what was needed was something which would not only bring some sense of unity, cohesion and coherence to the diocese itself but also encourage parishes to begin to look forward rather than backward (to the supposedly good old days!), and to help them identify and deliver some modest and realistic priorities for mission.

The 'MAP' process (Mission Action Planning) is well described by Mark Ireland and Mike Chew in this excellent book and I am enormously grateful that they have taken the time and the care to enquire more deeply both into the process and into some of the outcomes now in a number of dioceses.

I would never wish to claim too much for the 'MAP' initiative; furthermore I would never wish to impose too tight a straightjacket on its implementation – each diocese is different and each diocese, as with each parish, cluster, locality – call it what you will – will hopefully find this book helpful, useful and encouraging and adapt its content in seeking to further the mission entrusted to the church in every place and in so many different and varied settings.

One of my hopes would be that from this 'bottom-up' approach, as it were, listening to the priorities arising form the parishes and other places where the Church has a presence, it might be possible both to reorganize and restructure the organization of the diocese itself – even, dare I say it, of the Church of England nationally! For I am convinced, and not least in these present days and times, that we still need drastically both to lighten and to simplify the structures which can so often be a hindrance rather than a help to mission.

I am glad to be able to commend this lively and encouraging presentation by Mark Ireland and Mike Chew in the hope that it will both stimulate and challenge others to implement the process they describe, not simply as an end in itself, but rather by way of celebrating the many gifts God has given to each one of us, thus equipping 'the saints for the work of ministry, for building up the body of Christ, until all of us come to the unity of the faith and of the knowledge of the Son of God, to maturity, to the measure of the full stature of Christ' (Ephesians 4.12–13).

+David
Lord Hope of Thornes KCVO

Preface

A significant and growing number of churches in the UK and increasingly in other countries[1] are using the principles of Mission Action Planning (MAP). What is MAP? How do you do MAP? Is it just a management speak fad? Or is it an approach which is well grounded biblically and theologically? Is there any objective evidence from those parishes and dioceses which have used MAP that it is useful?

This is the first book which has been dedicated to MAP, and the process for producing a high-quality plan. It argues the case for producing a MAP, describes a practical ongoing process, gives practical examples, and provides evidence of the effectiveness of the process. It is based on research conducted in several dioceses of the Church of England – at diocesan and parish levels. The book is intended for clergy and lay leaders of churches – large or small – of all traditions.

There are many books published in the private and public sectors about developing strategy and improvement plans; and also many books have been published in recent years about the mission of the Church. This book is an attempt to bring these two strands together, written by people with experience in secular management and local church leadership.

1

Setting the scene

What is MAP?

A 'Mission Action Plan' is a document which outlines the mission activities that a local church is going to do in the coming months and years. It is built on a clear sense of God's 'vision' for the church – what God is calling the church to be and to do. So a MAP provides exactly what it says on the tin – an action plan for mission. Churches have been doing this for years, but most have found that the work involved is not as easy as it sounds. For a start, what is meant by 'mission'? How does a busy church decide on priorities? How does a traditional church prepare its people for doing new things? How does a church council agree and manage the many actions that may ensue?

What we are talking about here is strategic planning – something which businesses, schools, hospitals and most other organizations have to address every year. This is crucial work for them – if they get it right, they can thrive; if they get it wrong, they may face problems. They certainly don't carry on as they are – because 'business as usual'[1] will mean that they will probably miss opportunities and will underperform. To an outsider, the work may seem very obvious, but for a member of the board or management team, it is likely to be the hardest work that they do. Research is needed, reviews have to be conducted, options must be explored, priorities have to be assessed, resource plans must be made and decisions have to be taken.

Finally, detailed action plans can be drawn up: but that is not the end. There is a need to communicate to all stakeholders, and the methods for tracking progress must be worked out in advance. This 'strategic planning process' – the way of producing the strategic plan – is carefully managed by these organizations and the process is improved year by year. It is the largest market for business and management consultants.

What will a Mission Action Plan do?

A **MAP** makes sure the life and work of your church is:

- **Purposeful**
  - Doing what you are convinced is needed
- **Developing**
  - Always improving how you do these things
- **Focussed**
  - Not distracted by less important things.[2]

Every church has a vital role to play in building God's Kingdom, and therefore the same need for strategic planning – as a spiritual exercise – seeking to determine God's will for their future. In the church, however, all too often this is not given sufficient time in a busy programme – and there is a danger of becoming introspective, missing opportunities, taking on too much work because of a lack of priority planning, and overstretching a leadership team, made up largely of volunteers.

The church MAP is a summary of its mission strategy. It is tailored to the particular circumstances of the individual church, because it builds from the church Mission and Vision statements – its purpose and its desired future. Priorities are identified, and also those things which are not as urgent. The plans are kept alive by frequent reviews, and those involved can become enthusiastic about improving how they are serving God.

The MAP is a living document, and is usually communicated frequently to church members to build support for mission priorities, to invite people to pray for these, to encourage people to engage where help is needed and to prepare people for changes that are planned.

The method used to create a MAP – the MAP process – guides a church council through the hard work of producing a strategy for mission. It is divided into four phases: Review, Choose, Plan and Act. We introduce each of these later in this chapter, and they are covered in detail in Chapter 5.

Origins of MAP – David Hope

The origins of the phrase 'mission action planning' can be traced back to the arrival of David Hope in the diocese of London in the early 1990s. Faced with a huge diocese very divided over women priests and with acute money problems, Bishop David devised Agenda for Action, to establish four agreed mission priorities for the diocese. These were:

1 Worship and Prayer
2 Care and Service
3 Teaching and Nurture
4 Mission and Evangelism.

The staffing and finances of the diocese were then extensively refocused (with the loss of some diocesan boards and councils) to resource these mission priorities at local level. Each deanery and parish was then invited to follow a similar process, and to choose a few realistic targets which they wanted to set themselves in the light of the overall diocesan vision. Bishop David wanted to hear what people 'on the ground' wanted to do, so he invited parishes to send their plans to him. He planned to use their responses to further reshape the diocesan structures. For example, he noticed that some very good work with young people was going on in different places, and asked whether it was possible to bring the leaders together to share and learn from each other, and to offer advice for other parishes – but not to create a central structure. In other areas of parish work also, he wanted groups from strong parishes to help weaker ones. His overall aim was to help people to get away from thinking of internal domestic things and move on to become a church on the move – a pilgrim people travelling light.

Early in his time as Bishop of Wakefield, David Hope attended a course on leadership and teams, led by business guru John Adair,[3] which he found inspiring. Adair's seven marks of a high-performance team particularly got him thinking about how to lead a diocese and how a local minister could lead a church into mission work. The marks highlighted were:

1 Clear realistic objectives
2 Shared sense of purpose
3 Best use of resources
4 Atmosphere of openness
5 Reviews progress
6 Builds on experience
7 Rides out storms together.

Listening was a key part of David Hope's strategy. Spending time in the parishes, he encouraged them to be realistic about what they could achieve. He felt that the diocesan structure was a massive empire which needed to be dismantled, and after a process of visiting every deanery and listening to the parishes to learn what they believed they were being called to do, he then set about the task of restructuring the diocesan organization to serve the emerging vision. Putting resources back into the parishes through grants and local advisers meant taking them away from other areas, including industrial mission. One of his key phrases was 'prune for growth'.

David Hope's approach is interesting in that he encouraged a two-way dialogue, writing personally to those who had completed MAPs, and producing a report after the first year, feeding back to the parishes what they had said. Acknowledging that some parishes wanted nothing to do with MAP, he commented, 'We didn't force it: I thought – if it was good, it would spread by word of mouth.'

A key part of the MAP initiative was the half-day visits by senior clergy to each parish and deanery, followed by a return on the following Sunday to lead the people in worship – so that the bishops and archdeacons were seen to be listening to them and alongside them in mission. The parishes' willingness to engage with the MAP process was in part a response to a personal relationship with the bishop or leader who had come to them. This incarnational 'alongside' dimension of David Hope's approach to MAP models something crucial about the leader as 'servant/coach' rather than as top-down manager, and helps to explain why 70 per cent of parishes responded to his invitation to produce a MAP, compared with the usual 40–50 per cent response to any request from the Bishop.

> The London thing was very rudimentary – I was feeling my way a bit. What I really wanted to achieve was to give the diocese some sense of cohesion and coherence in terms of mission, and to try to change the whole ethos of the diocese. People had become disheartened, and were keen for a fresh vision and a change from arguments about women priests and gay priests.

David Hope was only in London for four years before his move to York, but the MAP process he had initiated was continued by Richard Chartres. When interviewed, David Hope said he believed that mission action planning contributed significantly to reversing the downward attendance spiral in the diocese – 'It wouldn't have happened without MAP.'[4]

Growth of the MAP phenomenon

The diocese of Lichfield adapted and adopted the London MAP model as part of its new strategy *Going for Growth*.

Other dioceses quickly followed suit and now there are a growing number of dioceses that are using MAP (or similar approach) as part of their diocesan strategy (see Table 1.1).

In addition to those mentioned in the table, several other dioceses have contacted us for information about MAP and to share thoughts and ideas about Church Growth strategy. When David Hope moved to York as Archbishop, he took the concept of MAP with him. His experience there is discussed in Chapter 7. Now, almost half the dioceses in the Church of England have some sort of mission strategy initiative, and most of these use the term 'Mission Action Planning' as the key tool for individual churches.

Introducing the MAP process cycle

The MAP process provides the way in to MAP work – in order to answer the practical question, 'How do we produce a MAP?' At its most fundamental, the process phases are:

1 Review your situation
2 Choose future priorities
3 Make plans
4 Act on the plans

. . . with prayer running all the way through each phase. MAP work is strategic work: it's about the long-term future of the church; it's about church growth and development, perhaps doing new things, rather than the essential issues of maintenance. Therefore, the MAP work should be carried out by the leadership of the church – normally the minister and church council (or a sub-group from the council). This section contains a basic MAP process description – perhaps suitable for a church that is doing this work for the first time. In Chapter 5, we describe a more in-depth process which could be used as a whole, or in part to add to the basic process.

Table 1.1 Diocesan growth initiatives

Diocese	Start year	Website description	Main parish tool
London	1993	Agenda for Action	MAP
York	1999	Living the Gospel	MAP
Lichfield	2003	Going for Growth	MAP
Llandaff	2004	Mission Action Planning	MAP
Blackburn	2004	Going for Growth	MAP
Portsmouth	2004	Kairos	Kairos Process
Coventry	2005	Shaping the church for Mission	Eight Questions
Exeter	2005	Mission Action Planning	MAP
Leicester	2005	Mission Partnerships	Mission Partnerships
Southwell	2005	Shaping the Future	Mission Values, Challenges and Questions
Newcastle	2006	Mission Action Planning	MAP
Carlisle	2006	Survival to Revival	Deanery Deployment Planning
Chichester	2007	Putting mission on the MAP in Chichester	MAP
Norwich	2007	Committed to Growth	Growth Plan
Ripon/Leeds	2007	Together in Mission visits	Toolkit for Mission
Ely	2008	Mission Action Planning	MAP
Wakefield	2008	Transorming Lives in Wakefield Diocese	Tranformational Plan
Chester	2009	Growth Action Plan	GAP
Birmingham	2009	Mission Strategy	MAP
Guildford	2009	Growing Communities of Faith & Engagement	Self-evaluation resource

Phase 1 Review your situation

The first task is to see the church's current situation as God would see it: listing those things that are good and working well, and those things which are not so good. To do this it is useful to devise ways to listen in three directions:

1 listening up – to God,
2 listening in – to church members, and
3 listening out – to the local communities and networks that the church serves.

Write down a summary of strengths, weaknesses and opportunities.

The second task is to reflect on what is the main purpose of the church:

- Why does this church exist?
- What particular purposes does it serve?
- How does it relate to the community?
- What does it believe in?

Perhaps the church already has a 'Mission statement' – which captures a sense of these. If not, consider how you can produce a statement which everyone can support. This should be limited to one sentence. For example, 'Christ Church is here to share the love of Jesus Christ with all ages in this community.'

Phase 2 Choose future priorities

While Phase 1 is concerned with the present time, Phase 2 is all about the future. People may have many ideas about what the church could be doing, but resources are finite and choices have to be made. The first step is to describe a vision of what the church could become in five years. You want this to be God's vision for your church, so prayer is essential. You also want this to be an attainable vision – not an impossible dream. An example Vision statement might read: 'St Anne's will become a church community where all members are growing in faith and using their special gifts to spread Jesus' saving love.'

A good Vision statement, shared and taken on board by your people, can inspire everyone to work together towards their future, so it is crucial that the church leadership enthusiastically buy in to it. So here again, this is a task for the minister and leadership to do together.

The second step in this phase is to work out the priorities to achieve the vision. This is best done in two stages – first consider the long-term (five-year) priorities, and then break this down into the priorities for the next year. In this way, you will be able to review progress every year, and to identify the next priorities. It may be tempting to take on too much, so be cautious. It is a good idea to restrict the number of discrete strategic priorities to three for an average church, and less where resources are limited. This is also a good time to consider what activities could be stopped or trimmed – especially if these are not central to the church vision. Fianlly, write a goal statement for each of the first-year priorities, which defines specifically 'what' has to be achieved by 'when'.

Phase 3   Make plans

During the planning phase, each priority can be taken in turn and fleshed out into the main actions that are necessary to reach the goal. For example, if the goal is 'To introduce an Emmaus nurture course within the next twelve months', the action list could be:

What	Who	When
Raise funding and purchase materials	AB	by end June
Identify and train group leaders	Minister	by end September
Publicize the course and invite people to join	HJ	from May
Start groups	Leaders	in October

Notice that it helps to identify the person responsible for the action, and the timescale. These are the 'top-level' actions, suitable for including in the MAP summary report; each one of these could be broken down into more detail by the owner of the action at a later date.

The MAP summary report can now be written. It should contain the main details of each of the work done in the three MAP process phases, but it should also be fairly brief and easy to read – two sides of A4 is ideal. The report should be widely communicated, with copies made available for all church members and key members of the local community.

Phase 4   Act on the plans

This is where the practical work gets done. During the Act phase, it is vital that there are regular reviews of progress – perhaps at church council meetings – to ensure that the people involved are supported and encouraged in their work. It may be found necessary to revisit the plans in the light of work done so far. For completed actions, it is useful to review whether the desired outcomes have come to pass, and plan any follow-on work. Finally, give thanks and celebrate!

Is MAP just another management fad?

Some church leaders are cautious about introducing 'business tools' into church life – perhaps because in the past there has appeared to be incompatibly between a hard-edged 'bottom line' emphasis and human/faith considerations. However, it is interesting to note that secular business writers are increasingly incorporating Christian concepts into their approaches for leadership and strategy development. For example, the business strategy process step of developing a clear Vision has origins in the Old Testament. The servant/coach style of

Leadership – which many business writers have identified as appropriate for today – aligns well with Jesus' example and teachings. In their book *The Leadership Challenge*[5] Kouzes and Posner reported on research into public and private organizations with regard to what values are admired in leaders by their staff. They found that top of the list were: honesty, vision, inspiration, competence, fair-mindedness and being supportive.

As we will see in Chapter 3, 'vision', 'planning' and 'action' are also solid biblical concepts, but often secular organizations have developed better ways of working – processes and tools – for determining the most appropriate plans and acting on them than we have in the Church. There is a distinction between management 'processes' and 'tools'. The leaders of organizations learn to use processes (or 'methods') to achieve their objectives and they strive to improve these as time passes. They learn from their own experience of what works best and from research carried out by universities, schools of management and consultants. Examples of key processes are:

- Strategic planning
- Budgeting
- Recruitment
- Market research
- Manufacturing method
- Performance Review.

The tools that are used within these processes may change through time, as improvements are introduced and new ways are discovered. For example, the tool 'Benchmarking' was introduced in the 1990s as part of the strategic planning process, and has stood the test of time; the tool 'Customer Surveys' gained popularity from the 1980s and became the norm in the 1990s. 'Management by Objectives' (MBO) was introduced in 1970 as a tool for management performance planning and review, but became unfashionable in the 1990s. So the need for management processes is constant and they are researched and improved through time, whereas specific tools can come and go. Mission Action Planning is a process, similar to strategic planning in the secular world, and therefore there will always be a need for it. It may be called different names by different churches or dioceses, but it is not a passing fad!

Who are we to comment?

The authors came together at St John the Baptist Church in Baxenden – when Mark Ireland was vicar there from 1989 to 1997, and Mike Chew was churchwarden for most of those years. This was Mark's first incumbency, and Mike's second spell as churchwarden. They shared a common passion – to spread the good news of the gospel and God's love. Mike was working for a well-known international company as a Business Excellence Manager and was keen to apply the principles of improvement strategy and leadership team building to the church. As you will see in the case study in Chapter 2, through God's grace there was substantial growth in faith and attendance at St John's, despite some mistakes.

In 1997, Mark left St John's to become the Diocesan Missioner for Lichfield diocese, where he invited Mike to help with strategy formulation and parish consulting. In his nine years as Diocesan Missioner, Mark worked with a whole variety of churches of all traditions, urban and rural, as they sought to develop a strategy for evangelism and mission. He also led a team of officers in the diocese, bringing together specialists in world mission, worship, spirituality, ecumenism, interfaith issues, social responsibility and industrial mission. One of the fruits of their work together was a new diocesan strategy, 'Going for Growth', designed to address the long-term decline of the diocese's ability to grow the Kingdom of God because of its declining and ageing membership. During his final year as missioner, Mark became also responsible for the Ministry division in the Lichfield diocese.

In the meantime, Mike had been promoted to the most senior position in his company, of international 'Business Excellence Director', but in 2000, after three years in the role, he decided that he needed to redress his work–life balance and left the company to set up his own consultancy business, but he continued to offer voluntary consulting for the Church. In 2004, Mike was invited by the new Bishop of Blackburn – Nicholas Reade – to join a new group that he was setting up to introduce Mission Action Planning in the diocese. From 2006, Mike also worked with the Bishop's Staff as Growth Strategy facilitator, and Team-Building coach. Also in 2006 and 2009, Mike led a workshop on MAP at the UK Missioners' conference, with support from Mark.

In 2006, Mark was appointed as vicar of All Saints, Wellington with St Catherine's Eyton – more about this in sub-sequent chapters.

In 2007, Mike met Peter Hill from Lichfield diocese, who had started a Ph.D. research project into MAP, and together they realized that there was a requirement from dioceses and other church organizations to share MAP experiences and approaches. Accordingly, they teamed up with another former churchwarden from Baxenden – Roger Longworth – to create and maintain the website: <http://www.churchmaps.co.uk> which has proved to be very popular. In September 2008, they organized a national 'MAP Study Day' at Mark's church in Wellington for people to meet and exchange experiences and ideas. Representatives from 14 dioceses and a representative of the Methodist Church attended.

This book brings together our experience of working on Mission Action Planning with parishes and dioceses, our research into the use of MAP as a tool by churches and dioceses across the country, and also our reflections on our own personal experience of strategic planning in our own local churches – from our different perspectives as business leader and churchwarden, vicar and missioner.

In the next chapter, we earth our discussion by reflecting on the years we worked together as churchwarden and vicar in a Lancashire parish in the 1990s.

2

Reflecting on our experience –
at St John's, Baxenden

Beginnings

RECOLLECTIONS BY MIKE CHEW

In 1989, Mark Ireland was appointed vicar of St John the
Baptist Church in Baxenden, a dormitory village on the south
side of Accrington in Lancashire, where I was one of the churchwardens. We feel that the Baxenden story is worth telling,
because these years were seminal to our thinking and learning
about mission in the local church and how to translate plans
into action.

Baxenden is a semi-rural village with a population at that
time of about 4,000, and usual Sunday attendance (uSA) for
three services at the church was about 170. Previously, the population of the village had reduced to around 2,000 in 1967, with
a uSA of 38; but then the first of three modern private housing
estates was built, and Mark's predecessor, Brian Harding – who
began his ministry in 1968 – had introduced a number of outreach initiatives.

The ministry of Brian Harding: 1968 to 1988

The small congregation had a kind of survival culture at that
time, because the diocesan officers had indicated that the
church was not viable and may have to close. However, they
didn't really know what to do. Brian's motivation was to be

Figure 2.1 St John the Baptist Church, Baxenden

obedient to the Great Commission,[1] and his strategy for the early years was simple but effective: to reach with the gospel the young families who were moving into the new houses through:

- Much prayer and a faithful witness
- Listening to God and being alert to the promptings of the Holy Spirit
- Church school contacts
- Sunday School and Pathfinder groups
- A group for mums and toddlers, led by Brian's wife, Branwen
- A monthly family service, which also involved the uniformed organizations.

. . . and to encourage growth in faith by:

- House groups, led by Brian, and others he invited
- Preaching from the Bible.

Brian felt that he needed to be the Chair of school governors in order to strengthen the links with the school – children, staff and parents. He decided that it was necessary to 'clear the site', as it were, for new building, by assessing how to direct people's thinking into Godly ways rather than worldly attitudes impinging on the core activity of the church.

Brian and Branwen were exited about the church's potential, and prayed that others would share this. They had many ideas, but waited patiently for the right time to talk about them. Interestingly, when they had a conviction that God wanted particular changes, they waited patiently until others suggested them: for example, the introduction of Family Services and the Alternative Services.

The workload was heavy, and there were many tears and setbacks. So Brian laid down some firm foundations for the future by developing a lay leadership team, which he relied on for sharing the workload and for support. Initially the leadership team was Brian, Branwen and the churchwardens, but later this evolved as the 'Ministry Team', and also included the coordinator of the childrens' groups, the pastoral care coordinator and a teacher who Brian felt might develop a call to leadership (and he later did).

The churchwardens were responsible for the building, and they built up a skilled team of helpers – mainly the husbands of the women in the mums' group. Several major projects were undertaken by these volunteers, including redecorating, installing new lighting and a sound system, removing some rear pews, moving the font, building a dais at the front of the church, and refurbishing the bells and steelwork in the tower. Brian was involved in all other areas of ministry – working extremely hard.

In 1980, an ecumenical monthly celebration service was introduced, attended by like-minded Methodist, Baptist and Free Church people. Talented musicians from these churches taught new songs, and people found a new freedom in worship.

To allow the Holy Spirit even more space, Healing and Prayer Ministry Services were introduced in 1982 and many people received ministry. This prepared the way for involvement with Mission England in 1984, and many people found a deeper faith. A major influence at that time was the emergence of the charismatic movement affecting people's perspective and a growth in sharing and every-member ministry. In particular, the leaders were responding to the continual guidance by the Holy Spirit through the involvement of lay leaders, and the use of leadership ideas from the secular world.

However, it wasn't all plain sailing – tensions developed between the older, more traditional members and the 'new' people. The former were happy with the church returning to life, but were uncomfortable with the physical changes to the building, and the changes to the worship pattern and style. The latter preferred more modern forms of worship and wanted activities for young people and informal midweek meetings to study the Bible. There were also financial problems, and these were made more acute by the discovery of dry rot in two areas of the church. Nevertheless, there was a definite feeling that people were growing in faith, and there was a steady increase in the number of worshippers. The team put this down to:

- putting God first, and being open to the leading of the Holy Spirit in prayer;
- from this, working out a clear vision for the church;
- working on priorities – and not getting deflected by day-to-day problems;
- good communication, leading to people volunteering to becoming involved.

The increase in attendance was very encouraging (see Figure 2.2), but the team had noticed that there had been a levelling out in the usual Sunday attendance (uSa) from 1983 – a plateau had been reached. Brian's ministry ended in 1988, after a very fruitful 20 years, when he moved to Christ Church, Parbold.

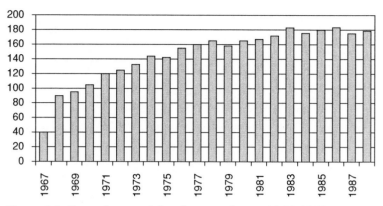

Figure 2.2 Baxenden usual Sunday attendance: 1967–1988

During an interregnum of eight months, the ministry team were able to continue the work he started, with no reduction in activities or attendance.

Baxenden from 1989: The start of Mark Ireland's ministry

Mark came to Baxenden – his first incumbency – in April 1989, as a single man prepared to work hard for growth of the Kingdom, both in terms of faith maturity and numbers of people. He asked the ministry team to continue in their work, while he focused on worship and got to know the people, the village and the way things worked. This period also gave him the opportunity to work out how he could lead the people to take the next steps.

Mark was a very popular vicar, and he worked hard on getting to know people and on the content of Sunday worship. He introduced new ways of teaching, often demonstrating biblical truths with drama. For two years, there was a period of rapid growth, but then a new plateau was reached. It occurred to Mark that a 'glass ceiling' had been encountered, where further growth was limited by the leadership structure and effort.

All operational decisions were taken by the vicar, and the whole ministry team. In addition, people were used to having personal contact with the vicar for all issues, and he was expected to be seen and available in the village. Also, there was no clear delegation structure, apart from responsibility for the building, taken by the churchwardens. So there was a kind of bottleneck effect, and the workload for the leader and leadership team was very high.

Furthermore, financial planning was also a problem, mainly because there was no annual budget. The treasurer of the time saw his main role as that of close management of the cash on a week-by-week basis. He questioned the value of producing a budget, when the money was not there in the first place. Rather, he preferred to see how much money came in through collections each week, and then allocate cash on a priority basis.

Mark called a special meeting of the ministry team to share his observations and thoughts about the present and future. He started by thanking the team for their hard work, and for their friendship and generosity to him during the first months. His main observations were:

- After recovering from the threat of closure, followed by a period of growth, people still seemed unsure about the future direction of the church, and its current priorities.
- Evangelism seemed to be the vicar's job, assisted by one or two members of the ministry team; whereas all are called to share their faith by using their particular gifts.
- The pastoral care work, including sick-visiting, was also the vicar's job, supported by a small team.
- The outreach to young families had been very successful, but there were few other examples of outreach to the wider community.
- The relationships between the church and other village networks – for example the pubs and shops – were rather underdeveloped.

- The relationships with the uniformed organizations were poor – there had been some past disagreements between the uniformed leaders and church leaders.
- The number of people involved in house groups was low.
- There were tensions between the ministry team and PCC (Parochial Church Council), because the method of appointment of members, their responsibilities and period of service were not clear.

The team talked about the 'glass ceiling' effect – that the effectiveness of the church was limited by the availability of the vicar and key leaders, especially relating to new people. Further, there was no structure for the delegation of work and decisions, and the absence of a clear understanding of priorities was exacerbating this situation.

Mark then went on to explain his immediate plans for the future:

1 To dissolve the current ministry team.
2 To define a new task-oriented structure, with clear job descriptions, responsibilities and accountabilities, with the agreement of the PCC.
3 To develop a draft Mission statement for the church – for PCC discussion and approval.
4 To appoint a new ministry team after consultation with the PCC and other church members.
5 To respond to the Bishop's request to carry out a Mission Audit.

Mark thanked the current team on behalf of the whole church, and invited them to help in this process. The result was a clear structure for the new ministry team, made up of people responsible for:

- Worship (the vicar)
- Children and Youth
- Outreach

- Building: maintenance and development (churchwardens)
- Pastoral care.

Some weeks later, after careful consultation and discussion in the PCC, each of these functions was defined. The ministry team role as a whole was defined as 'Vision and Application', and the PCC responsibility for Finance and Policy remained as before. People were invited to fill these roles, and not surprisingly, the new team was largely made up of the former ministry team members, but now with clearer roles.

A new Mission statement

The Mission Audit work provided a good framework to work out the priorities for the coming years, and a new Mission statement was agreed by the PCC:

> St John's exists to worship God, to win people for Christ and to help them witness in the world.

For each priority, an action plan was produced, and this was regularly reviewed by the new ministry team.

The next few years were a time of optimism, healing of relationships, outreach, quality teaching, house groups, youth work and care of the sick and elderly and, above all, an emphasis on prayer and holiness. Teams were appointed to assist the leaders of the main areas of ministry, and people were keen to be involved. The ministry team felt that the Holy Spirit was doing a great work amongst all the people.

The ministry team worked well together, and met every week. Church membership grew, and usual Sunday attendance topped 300 in 1994 (see Figure 2.3). However, there were challenges ahead . . .

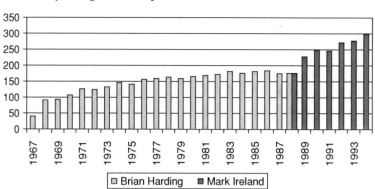

Figure 2.3 Baxenden usual Sunday attendance: 1967–1994

Baxenden from 1990: The new ministry team

RECOLLECTIONS BY MARK IRELAND

For me as a new and young vicar (appointed at 28) it was fascinating to listen to my churchwarden Mike reflecting on his experience as a quality manager in a well-known international company. In his working life he was seeking to drive a process of improvement and business excellence in order to stay ahead in an increasingly competitive environment, and in his church life feeling frustrated by a culture of doing the same old things in the same old amateurish way, and by the total lack of concern in the diocese at its declining membership. Mike helped me to imagine how church could be done better, doing things differently by listening to God and listening to people, and learning from our experience and mistakes. As he told stories from his work in occasional sermons and in meetings of the ministry team, we began to share a vision to glorify God by improving the quality both of our worship and our organization as a church. We didn't have the vocabulary then, but instinctively we were feeling our way towards a process of what we now call Mission Action Planning.

Some of my clergy colleagues regarded talk of planning and numbers as somehow unspiritual. However, mission is all about God, and the God of mission is calling us to act with him for the sake of the world. Looking back now at the attendance graphs for the parish of Baxenden, it is clear to me that growth in faith and numbers is God's work not ours, but that our work as church leaders is to clear away the blockages which stunt the growth potential of a godly and prayerful local church. Growing churches come up against a series of very tangible glass ceilings – after a period of growth, the growth levels off and either the church finds a way through that glass ceiling and begins to grow again, or else it bounces off the glass ceiling and numbers begin to ebb.

The need to find a way through a glass ceiling demonstrates the importance and value of Mission Action Planning. Prayer, preaching and pastoral care are all vital, but, without planning, the church will eventually find its optimum size and stop growing – hindered not by any failure of the Holy Spirit but by our human failure to remove those blockages which restrict and hinder growth.

The attendance graph for the eight and a half years I was vicar of Baxenden (see Figure 2.4) shows how we came up against three clear glass ceilings, and how (by God's grace) we managed to find a way through two of them, but failed to break through the third near the end of my time. When Mike showed me this graph again, 11 years after leaving the parish, I began to ask God what was significant about the events around each of those three periods.

The congregation grew rapidly in my first 18 months as vicar, having plateaued three years or so before, at the end of Brian's time. In my mind this spurt of new growth was clearly linked both to Brian's decision shortly before he left to establish a ministry team, to share responsibility for leading the parish, and to one of the first decisions I made when I arrived. The new ministry team had really come into its own (and earned its

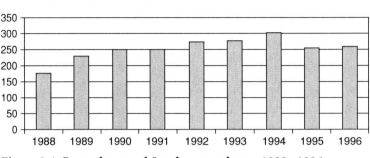

Figure 2.4 Baxenden usual Sunday attendance: 1988–1996

spurs in the eyes of the congregation) during the eight-month vacancy. The life of the parish had been maintained with minimal reliance on neighbouring clergy and, after an initial dip, numbers had begun to grow gently towards the end of the vacancy. When I arrived as vicar the team asked me if I wanted to take back the various roles that had been devolved to them, and at the same time various other church members came to see me about handing back roles that they had agreed to take on 'until we get a new vicar'. My instinctive answer to both groups was the same – 'Thank you for all you have done during the vacancy. I would be very grateful if you would continue in post and give me time and space to find my feet and to learn how things work here.'

The result was that the expansion of lay leadership precipitated by the vacancy continued, and I had the merciful space to listen, learn and be creative, rather than rushing in to cover all the good things that Brian had developed. The one area I took back to myself was responsibility for overseeing the worship and teaching. I was then able to invest time in starting a youth group, forming the first of a succession of enquirers groups, tidying the church building and beginning to give theological training to the emerging lay leaders.

Two years into my time as vicar, growth flattened out as we hit the next glass ceiling, and I found that my space to be creative was being squeezed out by the energy required to maintain the new things that had been created and to pastor the new people who had joined the church. Looking back, I believe four things helped us break through this glass ceiling eventually. First, having experimented with having a parish lay assistant, the parish then agreed to appoint a paid personal assistant who freed me from a great burden of administration (never my strong point!) and improved communication across the church. Second, we reviewed the role, function and accountability of the ministry team, increasing the sense of ownership by the PCC, giving each member a clear brief, and reducing the number of overlapping meetings. Third, we continued to broaden the number of theologically trained lay leaders – leading in time to the licensing of four Readers and six pastoral auxiliaries, as well as two ordinands being trained to serve elsewhere. Fourth, we undertook a parish-wide Mission Audit, at the invitation of the Bishop, to help us identify how we could better serve our local community by matching our strengths to its needs.

These important structural changes then laid the foundations for the next period of growth, from 1992 to 1994. This period of growth began with a personal visitation to every home in the parish – a remarkable achievement which was entirely lay-led, with a team of between 60 and 70 church members being trained by our pastoral team minister during Lent and then going out in pairs to visit every street during the early summer. Around this time we also formed a second pastoral team and several new house groups, in order to help us better disciple the growing number of worshippers.

After these years of growth we hit the third glass ceiling – the one we didn't manage to break through – in 1995 (see Figure 2.4). Again we reached a point where we had several capacity problems, hindering further growth. My workload as vicar had once more reached overload, and – feeling in need of both a rest and a new challenge – I decided to take a sabbatical working in our companion diocese of Bloemfontein, South Africa.

At the same time, having struggled for years with a building without proper facilities for midweek use and an increasing shortage of seating for Sundays, we were suddenly offered the possibility of completely reordering our church building through a very generous legacy. In July 1995, I came back from a very refreshing three-month absence in time to oversee the closure of our church building for a difficult seven-month period which led – in time – to a beautifully restored building opening up great new opportunities for worship and mission.

Interestingly, however, the building project led to a drop rather than an increase in attendance. By the time I left the parish 18 months later we still had not recovered the attendance levels prior to our temporary move into the cramped school hall. I am still pondering the reasons for this. Major building projects absorb an enormous amount of time and emotional energy, as people are very attached to buildings, even those with obvious problems. Not having to raise the money was a huge help on the one hand, but meant that the changes made were not necessarily owned by church members who had not had to raise the money to pay for them. If I were to do this again I would want to spend more time on the planning stages for the project, and more time working out how to use the temporary absence of the building creatively to move forward the worship and mission, rather than trying to minimize disruption by keeping everything as much as possible as it had been – and then moving people back into a building very different from what it was before. However, holding people together through such a process takes a lot of time and emotional energy – and is not possible when one is 6,000 miles away in the middle of it all!

Reflecting back on the experience of those nine years in Baxenden convinces me afresh of the value and importance of a robust pattern of Mission Action Planning for any parish. And each of those three words is vital. Glossy plans on a desk will achieve nothing unless breathed through with God's *mission* and backed up by concrete *action*. But equally, active mission-minded people will soon get frustrated by lack of results, and hurt their heads banging against a glass ceiling, if there is not a clear process of discerning God's will and *planning* for the growth he intends.

God is at work longing to bless his church with growth in holiness and new disciples. Our task is to discern how and where he is at work, and to remove the man-made blockages which hinder and get in the way. As St Paul says, 'I sowed the seed, Apollos watered it, but God made it grow' (1 Corinthians 3.6, NIV).

Baxenden from 1990

RECOLLECTIONS BY MIKE CHEW

Growth continued, but with it came a re-emergence of issues relating to the roles and busyness of the ministry team. Members were coming to the end of their period of service, and the next phase needed to be planned for. After a three-month period of prayer and discussion, the way forward became clear and Mark also benefitted from his experience as a member of a diocesan working group on collaborative ministry. The key points were:

1 To work out a new five-year 'Vision statement' for the church. The Mission statement had enabled people to understand their purpose, and what was expected of them, but it was not enough to clarify for all people what was important for the church and community. What was needed was a short sentence to communicate the aspirations for the future – so that people could continuously refer to it in order to keep them together – on the path towards the future. Although the ministry team's role had been described as 'vision and application' we had not articulated what the vision was.

2 To use the Vision statement to work out priorities, annual goals and an action plan that would steer the church towards its five-year vision. Actions would be allocated to the persons responsible for the appropriate areas, and a timescale would be agreed.

3 To communicate well to all people, using all available means on a regular basis.

4 To reinforce the role of the ministry team as being:
   (a) to prayerfully seek God's will for the parish;
   (b) to build up one another in love in our different gifts as apostles, prophets, evangelists, pastors and teachers;
   (c) to equip each member of our church for ministry, supporting them and enabling them to develop their gifts.

5 To prepare the way for this in practice by:
   (a) releasing leaders,
   (b) devolving responsibility,
   (c) improving communication.

However, a problem arose from a surprising source. A very large legacy had generously been left to the church: great news, but the issues here were related to gaining agreement about what to spend it on, the subsequent design, the management of the work and ensuring that the trustees of the donor estate were involved and happy with the plans and progress.

The church building would have to be closed for seven months while this work was completed, and the plan was to use the adjacent primary school for most Sunday services, and the local secondary school for the monthly family service. Also, Mark was due to take a sabbatical break, and was going to be out of the country for three months. The ministry team encouraged him to go ahead with this, but it meant that discussions about the project with the donors would have to be completed in the four months before he went away. The PCC supported Mark's plan to appoint a local project manager – a church member who was experienced in building project work – who would work with Mark to finalize details with the donors and the architect before the sabbatical, and then to deputize during Mark's absence. The churchwardens were not comfortable with supervising building work, so they were content with Mark's plan. At that time, I was working in The Netherlands, commuting home at weekends, and was not a member of the ministry team.

However, looking at Figure 2.4 it is clear that there were problems. We expected that attendance may fall when the church was closed for the building work, but even after reopening our beautifully restored and modernized church, recovery was very slow. On reflection, a number of issues contributed to this:

- The building project took a lot of Mark's time and energy, especially at a period when he was planning for the sabbatical break. Inevitably some areas of his ministry suffered.
- Due to time pressure, and also in compliance with the donor's wishes, the number of people involved in decision-making was very low. The PCC did not own the project.
- During Mark's absence, the ministry team were not involved at all in the project, and so communication to church members and the wider community was poor.
- The churchwardens were members of the 8 a.m. congregation, and were not as well known by the 10.15 a.m. people; this further complicated communication to the wider church.
- We neglected some further aspects of a good change management process:
  - Church members did not link the re-ordering work in the church with a vision of the future.
  - We lacked an effective leadership during the planning or execution stages of the project: not only the absence of Mark, but also a leadership team that could promote two-way communication with people. John Kotter would describe this as 'the guiding coalition'.[2]

- Our temporary facilities – the local school buildings – were too small, and some people decided to attend other churches; fringe members may have lost the habit of attending church.

Conclusions from the Baxenden Case

Looking back now over the Baxenden experience, we realize that there were some important lessons – some hard earned.

- The need to listen – to God through continuous prayer, to the community and to each other.
- The need for solid Bible-based teaching.
- The importance of understanding what is meant by 'church', and the purpose of the church, and to capture this in a good *Mission statement.*
- The importance of discerning where God is leading the church in the future, and communicating this in a Vision statement.
- In the early years in Baxenden, people prayed hard and worked hard together on 'survival' and mission work, but as time passed, another inspirational picture of the future was needed in order to keep people working together on the real priorities – discerning God's vision.
- The need for an annual action plan – based on priorities derived from a longer-term vision, with SMART actions (Specific, Measurable, Achievable, Resourced, Time-phased).
- The importance of having regular reviews of progress – including an honest, open look at what things were going well, and what things were not going so well, and what opportunities existed. The Mission Audit provided this in 1991, and, subsequently, an annual SWOT analysis was carried out (Strengths, Weaknesses, Opportunities and Threats).
- The need to have a good leadership team and structure, with responsibilities and expectations defined.

- The need to engage the PCC in policy decisions and for PCC members to be involved in the wider communication to church members.
- The need for excellent communication: between leaders and to the whole congregation.

3

Theological reflections on MAP

MARK IRELAND

Planning and prayer in Scripture

When we asked David Hope whether he felt MAP was just a good idea borrowed from the world of business, or whether it had a coherent theological rationale behind it, he responded immediately by pointing to the Pastoral Epistles and explaining: 'We are told that in order to be a good steward of the household of God, you have to be a good steward of your own household. It's really a dimension of stewardship – you have to plan and organize things. If we are serious about mission and that is the clear priority, then we've got to be business-like, and some sort of plan is inevitable.' However, Hope also acknowledged that the Holy Spirit has a habit of overturning things: 'Sometimes when you are making your plan, something comes in from the side wind and turns it upside down – that's the work of the Holy Spirit.'

Although influenced by Adair's ideas on leadership, Hope rooted his own approach in prayer and spirituality. In York the MAP process was begun with a whole year focused on prayer and worship, reading the Scriptures and waiting on God in prayer, with the publication of a series of guides, the *Archbishop's School of Prayer, Archbishop's School of Bible Study*, etc. so that planning was very clearly in the context of time given to prayer and discerning the will of God. Hope believes that faith is caught rather than taught, but said that in his experience people are attracted to join a lively fellowship where there is a clear sense of purpose and direction.

For David Hope, MAP is primarily a tool to establish a clear missionary purpose and direction for the Church. Far from being 'unspiritual', he sees planning as being of the very nature of God, whose character is seen in his plan in creation and in his plan of salvation for the world through Jesus Christ. Furthermore God has a plan or calling for each of our lives, in order that we might fulfil his purpose for us.[1]

Although David Hope may have coined the term 'Mission Action Planning' in the 1990s, the concept of planning for mission is hardly an original idea . . .

In Luke's Gospel Jesus demonstrates a carefully planned mission strategy when he trains and sends out the Twelve from village to village to preach and heal, and then trains up and sends out a larger number on a similar mission to prepare the ground in the places he himself was about to visit.[2] Jesus also takes for granted careful planning before undertaking any important task when he encourages his listeners to count the cost before deciding to follow him:

> For which of you, intending to build a tower, does not first sit down and estimate the cost, to see whether he has enough to complete it? . . . Or what king, going out to wage war against another king, will not sit down first and consider whether he is able with ten thousand to oppose the one who comes against him with twenty thousand?[3]

Planning is a word that comes up in a number of places in Paul and Acts – for example in Romans 15.24 where Paul is on his way to Jerusalem, but is then planning to visit Rome on his way to Spain. However, Paul's plans often had to change, in response to events or to fresh guidance from God – a useful reminder to us today that a MAP has to be a working document, constantly updated.

Prayer and supernatural guidance are key parts of planning for mission in the early Church. For example in Acts 13.2–3:

> While they were worshipping the Lord and fasting, the Holy Spirit said, 'Set apart for me Barnabas and Saul for the work to which I have called them.' Then after fasting and praying they laid their hands on them and sent them off.

However, discerning the leading of the Holy Spirit isn't always that easy – later, in Acts 16, Paul has a frustrating time trying to discern God's leading. Forbidden by the Holy Spirit to speak the word in Asia, he tries to enter Bithynia, only to be prevented by the Spirit of Jesus, before eventually having a vision of a man from Macedonia pleading for him to come over and help him.[4] Peter's life-changing encounter with the Roman officer Cornelius in Acts 10 is another example of God's unexpected guidance not only changing Peter's plans but also his whole way of thinking.

Over 25 years of ordained ministry I have made many plans for mission, but often the most significant works of God have been quite unplanned or unforeseen. For example, as a young (but not at all sporty) curate a 'chance' encounter with some older teenagers from the estate in the local park led to the forming of relationships, which led in time to me forming and running two church football teams. I knew next to nothing about soccer, and they knew nothing about Jesus, but we learned from one another and, as a result, several of them came to a living faith and were confirmed. Yet if anyone had told me before ordination that I would find myself organizing football teams (and even training as a referee) I would have run a mile!

Or again, one evening when I was a team vicar in Walsall, I noticed two Asian men sitting behind me in church. Going over to welcome them, I discovered that they were nurses recently arrived from Pakistan to work in the local hospital. Having spent a year teaching in Pakistan before ordination, I used the very few words of Urdu I could still remember to greet them, and invited them back to our home for coffee. My wife and I prayed with them, relationships began to form, and within a few months we had a brand new Asian congregation of around 40–50 people meeting in our church hall, and beginning to impact what had (up to then) been a fairly monochrome white congregation in the middle of a very multicultural town. God even provided an Urdu-speaking pastor, in the person of an Anglican priest married to one of the next nurses to arrive from Pakistan!

Both these examples remind me that mission is primarily God's work, not ours – we serve a missionary God who is at work in the world by his Holy Spirit, and he is the one who brings forth the harvest: 'I sowed the seed, Apollos watered it, but God made it grow . . .' (1 Corinthians 3.6). Or to put it another way, we must be like Jesus, who could do nothing by himself but only did what he saw the Father doing (John 5.19). This doesn't mean for one minute that making action plans for mission is unimportant. In fact the process of prayer and listening involved in the MAP cycle – as we seek to discern God's will – makes us more receptive to the unexpected guidance and prompting of God. A church which is committed to the MAP process is also one which is more likely to recognize and respond to the missionary work of the Holy Spirit.

Growing as a biblical image

The verb *auxano* (a strengthened form of *auxo*, to grow) is found 22 times in the New Testament. In the Synoptic Gospels the picture is of the plant-like growth of the Kingdom of God in the face of all opposition, through the seed of the word. God is the one who causes the growth of that which he himself has planted, through Jesus or through his servants. In Paul *auxano* is used of the growth of the Church despite human division as in 1 Corinthians 3.6. Only by remembering its origin in Jesus can the Church truly grow, and the growth that Paul envisages is both in numbers, in maturity and in communal life.[5] In Acts *auxano* is an important word for the missionary activity of the Church – as the word of God spreads so the number of disciples increases, as for example in 6.7, 'So the word of God spread. The number of disciples in Jerusalem increased rapidly, and a large number of priests became obedient to the faith . . .'

Removing hindrances to growth

I believe a key part of MAP is not just trying to foresee what God is going to do in the future, but trying to spot the ways in which current structures and patterns are hindering what God is doing today, and working out how to remove the blockages and release the growth which is the fruit of the Spirit's work among us. Too often God brings people into our churches, only for us to unconsciously drive them out again by our failures in organization and pastoral care.

This is one of the key insights of Christian Schwarz in his *Natural Church Development Handbook*.[6] Drawing on Mark 10.26–29, Schwarz articulates the 'all-by-itself' principle – that the seed, once planted in the ground, grows all by itself, though the farmer knows not how. Churches are living organisms, and living organisms that are healthy grow naturally – and so the work of church leaders (and of the MAP process) is to spot those obstacles and hindrances that restrict the God-given growth potential of the church.

Drawing on a vast body of research from churches world-wide, Schwarz has identified eight 'quality characteristics' which a church needs in order to grow. These are:

1 Empowering leadership
2 Gift-orientated lay ministry
3 Passionate spirituality
4 Functional structures
5 Inspiring worship services

6 Holistic small groups
7 Need-orientated evangelism
8 Loving relationships.

However strong a church may be in certain of these areas, its potential to grow will always be limited by the one weakest or 'minimum' factor. Schwarz uses a number of analogies from life and from natural processes to press home this point. For example, if a diet is generally good but deficient in one vitamin, ill health will result because of that one weakness regardless of how good the rest of the diet is. Similarly, crop yields in a field will be limited by whichever essential fertilizer is present in the smallest quantities.

The most helpful way to grasp how the 'minimum factor hypothesis' works is through the milk barrel image (see Figure 3.1). In Switzerland, milk has traditionally been kept in barrels made from vertical slats of wood. If these slats are of different lengths then the amount of milk that can be held will depend upon the height of the shortest slat. Barrel capacity can only be increased by making the shortest slat longer – any changes to other parts of the barrel are a waste of energy.

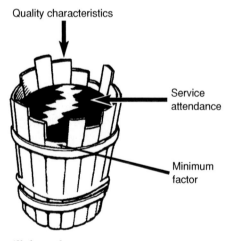

Figure 3.1 The milk barrel

For some church leaders this illustration has probably been the single most important learning experience in encountering NCD (Natural Church Development). The value of an NCD survey as a diagnostic tool within the 'review' stage of the MAP process is discussed in Chapter 5.

An obvious example in the New Testament of dealing with hindrances to growth is the appointment of the seven deacons in Acts 6. God-given growth in membership was producing administrative chaos, and one group in the church were being pastorally neglected. If this had not been addressed, division and disunity (fuelled by allegations of racism) would have been allowed to grow and the church would have been torn apart. Instead the Twelve gathered all the disciples together, addressed the issue, invited the church to appoint seven deacons to over-see this task (all, interestingly, were chosen from the previously neglected group), and the Twelve got back to their core task (of prayer and the ministry of the word). We read, as a result, that 'The word of God continued to spread: the number of the dis-ciples increased greatly in Jerusalem . . .'.[7]

Very often we are unaware of the obstacles we put in the way of those whom God is drawing to himself. When I was vicar of Baxenden the popularity of our Christingle service began to cause us problems. I have always been worried about the safety of lighted candles when lots of children are crowded into one place, and when attendance at our annual Christingle service began to top 350 we reluctantly decided (on grounds of health and safety rather than mission) that the next year we would hold two identical services (at 3.30 p.m. and 5.30 p.m.) and invite people to choose which service suited them. We had no way to predict how many would come to each service, and when a shade under 300 people turned up at the 3.30 p.m. service we thought we had failed and that there would be hardly anyone at the later service. However, to our amazement, another 300 people came to the 5.30 p.m. service! This made us realize just how many people in the community were wanting to come to church and were being put off by practical issues of space, car parking, safety and audibility. This led to a major rethink of how we catered for big occasions in the life of the church.

In my current parish we have begun to identify and address some clear limiting factors which hinder people joining the church and growing into discipleship. Two years ago we realized that the way we administer communion (with everyone from the gallery coming down to the communion rail) was a limiting factor – in a church that is proud of its preaching tradition we were actually giving more time to the distribution of the sacrament than to the sermon. Offering communion stations upstairs as well as downstairs was unpopular at first, but has helped the congregation to grow in numbers. The next limiting issues for us to overcome (at time of writing) are how to increase our administrative and office support, to enable us to care efficiently for a growing organization, and how to make more space for our children's and midweek groups.

More than numbers

Nonetheless, our effectiveness in achieving more disciples of Jesus Christ cannot be measured solely by more people attending church – we are seeking not just attenders but converts, and not just converts but disciples. Increasing the numbers in church is easy – if we put on more special events, pet services, Christingles, open up our policies on baptism and remarriage, and so on. However, these will not further the Kingdom of God one iota unless the new attenders are helped to become disciples of Christ and part of God's mission in the world.

However, numbers do matter. An end to the hitherto relentless decline in numbers attending church should be one important sign, among others, that a diocesan MAP strategy is bearing fruit – especially as research shows that, for the majority of Christians, belonging precedes believing: they begin to attend church and then gradually come to believe the gospel. Furthermore, in any voluntary organization the numbers who choose to participate in its activities is one indication of its health. Essentially, we are not seeking to grow the church for her own sake, but for the sake of Christ, whose bride she is. We also look for growth in the church because we long for more individuals to come to faith in Christ, and for the church to have a greater impact for God in the world, fulfilling her sacred calling to be 'a sign, agent and foretaste of the Kingdom of God'.[8]

A diocese that did not care about losing numbers would be no better than a parish that did not care about those who drifted away, or a shepherd that did not care about the lost sheep . . .

God's work of mission

In his magisterial book *Transforming Mission*, David Bosch begins with the assertion that up to the 1950s mission meant (a) propagation of the faith, (b) expansion of the reign of God, (c) conversion of the heathen, and (d) the founding of new churches.

> However all these connotations of the word mission are of fairly recent origin – until the 16th century the term was used exclusively with reference to the doctrine of the Trinity, that is the sending of the Son by the Father, and of the Holy Spirit by the Father and the Son.[9]

This is a helpful reminder that mission is fundamentally not a human activity, but a sharing in the divine work. 'Mission is participation in God's existence in the world.'[10]

The term 'mission' is so widely used in the Church and in the world today as to be in danger of losing its essential meaning of 'being sent'. However, as David Bosch reminds us, fundamentally mission belongs to God and must be understood in relation to the saving events of the life, death and resurrection of Jesus. Different strands of the Church have traditionally emphasized different events, but a holistic view of mission needs to incorporate them all:

1 The Incarnation – the life of Jesus of Nazareth challenges the Church to have compassion on the marginalized and to practise solidarity with victims in society.
2 The Cross – Christ died for our sins, and made forgiveness possible; without the cross at its heart Christianity would be a religion of cheap grace.
3 The Resurrection – the preaching of the apostles focused on 'Jesus and the resurrection'. In the Eastern Church it is the resurrection of Christ (rather than his death) which is God's saving act par excellence. The Church models the victory of Christ as a sign of contradiction against the forces of evil.
4 The Ascension – the ascension celebrates the rule of Christ as King. The Church is the present embodiment of God's reign, called to build civil society and work for the final con-summation of all things in Christ.
5 Pentecost – the Church continues Christ's mission in the power of his Spirit, making disciples and healing the sick, bold in the face of adversity and opposition.
6 The Second Coming – an awareness of the ultimate return of Christ should make the Church not a waiting room for eternity but the vanguard of God's reign. The Church is called to practise 'expectant evangelism', anticipating the day when Christ returns and the time of mission will be over.[11]

Mission and evangelism

The mission of God is, of course, wider than evangelism. In the fullest sense, mission is about being sent. God is already at work in mission through his Spirit in every life, every culture and every community. Christians, that is, those who follow Jesus Christ and his call to 'follow me', must follow that call in all its dimensions. God's desire for restored human relationships, for social justice, for a right relationship between human beings and the created world, are all part of that mission. But that cannot be the totality of the mission the Church is called to. There is also a call to make disciples, following the last command of Jesus to his followers as recorded in Matthew 28.19, 20:

> Go therefore and make disciples of all nations, baptizing them in the name of the Father and of the Son and of the Holy Spirit, and teaching them to obey everything that I have commanded you.

This great commission from the risen Jesus Christ is not a command recorded in one Gospel alone. All the other Gospel writers, albeit in different words and different settings, note the desire of Jesus that those who follow him should call others to follow too (Mark 16.15, Luke 24.47–49, John 20.21–23).

The mission of God is not being undertaken in all its fullness unless we are calling people to become disciples of Jesus Christ. Mission is not always evangelism, and some aspects of mission (responding to social injustice, for example) are very clearly not evangelism. Evangelism, then, is just one part, but it is nevertheless an essential and indispensable part of the mission of God. As Bosch puts it,

> Mission includes evangelism as one of its essential dimensions. Evangelism is the proclamation of salvation in Christ to those who do not believe in him, calling them to repentance and conversion, announcing forgiveness of sin, and inviting them to become living members of Christ's earthly community and to begin a life of service to others in the power of the Holy Spirit.[12]

Church as an instrument of God's mission

'The church on earth is by its very nature missionary' – Second Vatican Council.[13] The *Constitution on the Church* of the Second Vatican Council reminds us that the Church will attain her full perfection only in the glory of heaven, when the human race as well as the entire world will be perfectly re-established in Christ. Rising from the dead, Jesus sent his Spirit upon his disciples and through the Spirit has established his body, the Church, to be the universal sacrament of salvation. By sharing in the mission of the Holy Spirit, the Church is drawing people to Christ and preparing them for the promised restoration of all things.

The Church is called into being by God not for its own sake, but to be a sign, instrument and foretaste – that is a sacrament – of the Kingdom of God. This way of describing the Church has found wide ecumenical agreement, being expounded in the Anglican–Reformed agreed statement *God's Reign and Our Unity*, and in the ARCIC agreed statement *Church as Communion*.[14]

To quote from Bosch again:

> The church-in-mission . . . may be described in terms of sacrament and sign . . . It is not identical with God's reign yet not unrelated to it either; it is 'a foretaste of its coming, the sacrament of its anticipations in history'. Living in the creative tension of, at the same time, being called out of the world and sent into the world, it is challenged to be **God's experimental garden on earth, a fragment of the reign of God**, having 'the first fruits of the Spirit' (Rom. 8.23) as a pledge of what is to come (2 Cor. 1.22).[15]

Bosch's beautiful image of the Church as a garden intrinsically implies planning and design, for every gardener has a plan for what they are trying to create, and a plan that is constantly evolving. When we moved to a new parish two years ago my wife and I were rather daunted by the large and overgrown garden. One of the first things we did was to draw up a brief action plan, to help us identify short-term and long-term priorities, and to identify resources and people we needed in order to help us with the task – for example, buying a tractor mower, getting a team of tree surgeons to cut down and prune lots of trees, getting a builder to landscape the patio, and persuading my father-in-law to teach me how to organize a vegetable garden.

Mission-shaped Church

One of the most helpful features of the Church of England report *Mission-shaped Church* is its emphasis on values rather than mere activity in defining a missionary church. Those of us who are activist by nature have to beware the danger of thinking that becoming a mission-shaped Church is simply about doing new things – or doing *more* things! Instead, the report challenges us at a deeper level to think differently about everything that we do as church. The goal of the report is a 'mission-shaped Church', not simply a 'church-shaped mission'. The 'five values for missionary churches' form one of the most quoted and most useful sections in the report:

- A missionary church is focused on God the Trinity
- A missionary church is incarnational
- A missionary church is transformational
- A missionary church makes new disciples
- A missionary church is relational.[16]

When I was reflecting on these values in the context of developing a growth strategy for a diocese, I found that the order of the five values given needed some reworking.[17] The relational character of the Church rightly derives not simply from the fact that a community of faith is being formed, but from the Trinitarian character of God, the perfect expression of love-in-relationship. Just as the incarnation of the Son flows out of the inter-relationship of love in the Godhead, so the missionary church is incarnational in seeking to truly enter the communities it seeks to reach and in being born afresh among them, shaping itself in relation to the culture in which it is located. It is as the church becomes and reveals the body of Christ in a local community that people hear and respond to the call to become disciples. Finally, it is the new disciples who themselves help to transform the wider society with the values of God's Kingdom. Therefore, a more helpful order for these values is:

- A missionary church is focused on God the Trinity
- A missionary church is relational
- A missionary church is incarnational
- A missionary church makes new disciples
- A missionary church is transformational.

Taking the long view

In our thinking and planning it is important to keep the long view. In today's target-driven culture there is a subtle temptation to seek results that look good in the short term. Every time I enter the parish church I serve, I am confronted by the list of names of my predecessors, going back to 1189. This is a powerful and timely reminder to me that we are always building on another's foundation, and the enduring fruit of our labours will only be seen long after we have gone.

Three years ago I spent part of my sabbatical in the Egyptian desert, visiting the cave and monastery of St Antony the Great (AD 251–356). On hearing Jesus' words to the rich young ruler, Antony sold all he had, gave the money to the poor and devoted the rest of his life to prayer, gradually retreating further and further from the crowds into the utter desert.[18] The last decades of his life were spent alone in a tiny cave high up in the mountains, wrestling in prayer. When he died, there was little to show in terms of measureable result. Yet that one life of prayer has had as profound an impact on the history of the Church 1,700 years later as any other. His life inspired a whole generation of Desert Fathers and Mothers, and even influenced Benedict of

Nursia as he drew up his own *Rule* which shaped monasticism in the West.

Working for the long term will inevitably mean making decisions that may be painful or misunderstood in the present. In Jesus' own ministry recorded in the Gospels there are times of disappointment – as the rich young ruler walks away, as Jesus experiences rejection in his home town (Luke 4), as many disciples turn back from following him after the hard teaching in John 6, and as his remaining 11 disciples temporarily desert him in Gethsemane. In the life of Jesus we see times when he is followed by vast crowds, and also times when he is utterly alone. The example of Jesus is clearly one of faithfulness and challenging people to discipleship rather than seeking popularity and success.

Popularity and success – none of us in Christian leadership is immune from temptations, and it has been really important (and uncomfortable) for me to sit down from time to time with my spiritual director or companion, to seek to identify what are the motives that are really driving me. Am I really seeking disciples for Jesus and the growth of his Kingdom, or am I also worried whether people think I am doing a good job and leading a 'successful' church?

Johannes Verkuyl, Gailyn van Rheenen and others have written some important reflections on motivations for mission, distinguishing pure and impure motives.[19] At the conscious level we may think we are being driven solely by our gratitude for the gospel, our love and compassion for those without Christ and by our longing to bring an end to injustice and oppression. However, deep down our own insecurities may play a part – our need for affirmation, our desire to prove wrong those who might have written us off in earlier life, or our need to be needed.

Understanding and confronting our own impure motives can help us to keep focused on Christ alone, and not on what others think. For the only verdict on our ministry which ultimately matters is the one we won't hear until it is all over – 'Well done, you good and faithful servant.' And the only fruit which ultimately endures will be that we only see in the new creation – when we see among that great crowd whom no one can number gathered around the throne of Christ those whose lives have somehow been touched in some small way by ours.

4

How does MAP fit with other recent approaches to mission?

MARK IRELAND

————◆•◆•◆————

In Alan Smith's recent book, *God-shaped Mission*, he argues that one of the reasons for the lack of impact of the Decade of Evangelism was the lack of consensus over the causes of the decline of Christianity in the West, and consequently no agreement on how the Church should respond. For example, those converted by hearing a sermon may think the best (or even the only) way to evangelize is through preaching, whereas someone brought to faith through the beauty of the worship or music may put a high priority on quality of music or aesthetics.

Smith goes on to outline four groups of popular diagnoses and solutions, and to picture them as overlapping circles, representing issues of truth, issues of spirituality, issues of organization and issues of culture (see Figure 4.1).

Having followed Alan Smith as diocesan missioner in Lichfield diocese, my own experience of working with churches of all traditions resonates very much with this analysis. Too often we get hooked on just one of the circles as being the whole answer, without grasping the complete picture and realizing that all four circles are essential, and giving due weight to each one. If we focus all our energies on one area and neglect the others, our strategy will be unbalanced and growth will be hindered as a result – just as in Christian Schwarz's famous picture of the barrel in the *Natural Church Development*

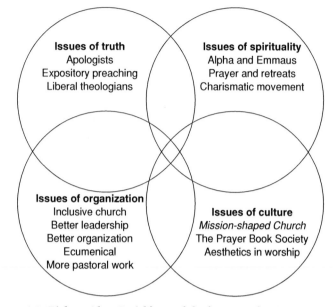

Issues of truth
Apologists
Expository preaching
Liberal theologians

Issues of spirituality
Alpha and Emmaus
Prayer and retreats
Charismatic movement

Issues of organization
Inclusive church
Better leadership
Better organization
Ecumenical
More pastoral work

Issues of culture
Mission-shaped Church
The Prayer Book Society
Aesthetics in worship

Figure 4.1 Bishop Alan Smith's model of approaches/groups

Handbook (see Figure 3.1 on p. 38); for the barrel to hold the maximum amount of liquid all staves of the barrel need to be of similar height.

For too long, some sections of the Church (both evangelical and liberal) have stressed issues of truth as paramount, wanting in their own ways to make faith credible, while failing to appreciate that however good their work in this area the Church may not grow if basic issues of organization have not been addressed – for example, if at diocesan level the policy of leaving churches vacant for longer to save money is still in place, even though this is the quickest way to shrink the membership; or at local church level the apologetics may be great, but if the notice board is misleading and the website six months out of date, then there may be no new people in church to hear the gospel unfolded.

Similarly, at time of writing, the incredible impact of the report *Mission-shaped Church* has challenged most Anglican and Methodist churches to think about the need to create culturally appropriate fresh expressions of church to enable them to reach those cultural groups not being impacted by traditional or inherited models of church. Many exciting new initiatives have resulted, with cutting-edge new Christian communities being formed among surfers in Cornwall and skateboarders in Nailsea, in 2001, in converted shops in the West Midlands and midweek after-school clubs, as well as age-specific outreaches among the elderly or among young people all over the country. However, it is the extent to which these fresh expressions of church actually enable the participants to engage with issues of truth – to hear the gospel in their own language and respond to it, and to be enabled in turn 'to give a reason for the hope that is within them' – that will determine whether they produce lasting fruit.

In Smith's model, Mission Action Planning clearly falls in the 'issues of organization' circle. MAP is a key tool in helping the Church to organize itself for mission and to plan strategically for growth. However, strategic organization is only one part of growing the Church and the Kingdom. A good MAP there-fore needs to measure itself against the other circles in the dia-gram – does the MAP help the Church to address those issues of truth, of spirituality, of culture and of social action that are essential if we are to grow mature disciples of Jesus Christ who are able to share in God's mission to his world?

While affirming Smith's central thesis, I would want to suggest some amendments to the categories he includes in each of his four groups. For example, while Alpha and Emmaus do have strong elements of prayer, belonging and openness to the Spirit, their primary focus is on teaching the truths of the Christian faith, and so I would suggest they better fit in the 'issues of truth' circle. Within Smith's second circle 'issues of spirituality' I would include the work of all those seeking to engage with the contemporary search for spirituality, finding ways to reach those who are very interested in the endless range of 'spiritual' things found in the 'mind, body, spirit' section of any bookshop – from horoscopes and tarot, to reflexology and aromatherapy – but who do not think of institutional churches as being in any way relevant to their spiritual searchings. Yvonne Richmond, Steve Hollinghurst and the CPAS (Church Pastoral Aid Society) *Essence* course all offer important insights into evangelism in an age of spiritual searching.

Within the 'issues of spirituality' circle I would also want to include the key question underlying any mission strategy, namely, 'Where can we discern the Holy Spirit at work today?' Our mission will always be more fruitful when we are able to spot God's own agenda for our church or community and seek to bless what he is doing, rather than laying out our agenda and asking him to bless that.

In the third circle, 'issues of organization', as well as including MAP I would also include church planting. The traditional methodology of church planting (seen in *Breaking New Ground*, the DAWN initiative[1] etc.) has been primarily an organizational approach – typically taking a leader and team from a strong church and using that either to form a new congregation in a formerly unreached area (a primary school on a new estate perhaps) or to bring new life to a dying or dwindling existing church. This approach has yielded significant results, especially in the 1980s and 1990s, though the more recent emphasis (in tune with *Mission-shaped Church*) has been on growing new culturally relevant expressions of church rather than on simple replication of an existing formula.

I would also suggest that there is a fifth group or circle which Smith has omitted, namely 'issues of social action/responsibility'. I am thinking here, for example, of the whole social responsibility agenda, the work of industrial mission and world development, all of which help to demonstrate the truth of the gospel, making it credible by the way in which it is lived out and demonstrated in the community. The earliest history of the Church shows that it was the early Christians' practice of caring for the dead and giving them a decent burial that began to make people in the Roman Empire think seriously about Christianity.

Similarly, a friend of mine has recently spent some time in Nanping in Fujian province (China) where it was the *demonstration* of God's character by social action (building an elderly care home) that persuaded the communist authorities that the church was doing something useful, and the ministry of healing persuaded various former communist officials that God was up to *delivering* change in a way that won their love and trust.

Amongst the wealth of recent work on social action and evangelism it is worth mentioning Ann Morisy's community ministry approach, the Church of England's follow-up report to *Faith in the City*, and Mark Green's work on being a Christian in the workplace.[2]

As an example of how focusing on only one circle is not enough, it is significant that Holy Trinity Brompton (HTB), as well as investing heavily in church planting and in promoting process evangelism through the Alpha course, has also in recent years developed a host of social action projects, including the Alpha in prisons initiative and the Besom project <http://www.besom.com>. The Besom project, founded by HTB member James Odgers, seeks to sweep away poverty and injustice by enabling those who have wealth and possessions to interact personally with those who haven't, in a way that changes the lives of both. For example, wealthy young professionals from South Kensington regularly give up their weekends to offer help to new tenants on sink estates to decorate and furnish their council flats.

Developing Smith's idea of four circles, I would therefore suggest a five-circle model as shown in Figure 4.2.

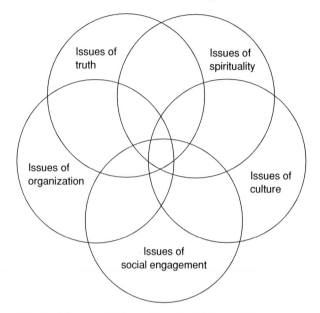

Figure 4.2 Building on Bishop Alan Smith's model

Issues of truth – Apologists, Alpha and Emmaus, expository preaching, liberal theologians

Issues of spirituality – What is the Spirit doing?, prayer and retreats, charismatic movement, search for spirituality/*Essence*

Issues of organization – *Hope for the Church/Road to Growth*, Mission Action Planning, church planting, ecumenism

Issues of culture – *Mission-shaped Church*, Prayer Book Society, aesthetics in worship

Issues of social engagement – social responsibility, industrial mission/faith at work, community ministry (Ann Morisy), HTB's Besom project, world development

Each of these five circles is vital if a church is to have a holistic and well-balanced approach to mission. Otherwise, if a church puts all its energies into only one or two circles, then the growth that might come through those strategies is likely to be dissipated by its weakness in other areas. For example, a church may have the highest quality evangelistic courses and preaching, but if it has no engagement with the social problems of its community then fewer people outside the church will be likely to see the church as either relevant or attractive, and some of those who do come to a living faith may in time drift to another church which better equips them to live out the gospel imperative for the poor.

Similarly, a church may develop a really creative fresh expression of church in a local Starbucks, or a ministry to skateboarders, which unchurched people find attractive and cool to attend, but unless there is a clear apologetic and call to discipleship, then when a person's social circle or hobby changes then they are likely to simply drift from church.

Another way to look at this five-circle model is to compare it to the staves on the milk barrel illustration coined by Christian Schwarz – mentioned earlier in this chapter. Just as what determines the amount of liquid the barrel can hold is the length of the shortest stave, and therefore what enables a church to grow is to address its one weakest factor, so it may be helpful to think of the five circles as staves in a barrel, and for a church (or a diocese) to identify which of the five circles it is weakest at, and consider how to address its weakness in that area in its MAP.

Suggested exercise

This five-circle model can provide a very helpful and illuminating template against which to compare a church's MAP. This can be simply done by explaining the five-circle diagram to a group or leadership team and then drawing a large set of five labelled circles on a flipchart, and asking the group to write in each circle what the church is doing or has recently done connected with the issues in each circle. Having done so, put the completed diagram in the centre of the group and allow a few minutes for silent prayer and reflection. Then ask the group to discuss what the flipchart reveals about the church's emphasis and priorities.

5

Producing a Mission Action Plan – step by step

MIKE CHEW

———◦◆◦———

The Starting Point

Prayer

We start with prayer – because all mission flows from God. It is through prayer that we seek the will of God, offer him our hopes and dreams and receive his vision and the strength for the way ahead.

While we take responsibility for mission, we know that, above all, we are participating in God's creative activity in the world. 'It's not the church of God that has a mission, but the God of mission who has a church.'[1] The Christian mission that is not founded on personal and corporate prayer is likely to be wasteful and ineffective. Before you start thinking about your own hopes for your church and your own ideas about its priorities, start by listening to God.

There are many ways of doing this. For example:

- Organize a day of prayer in the church, or a series of days.
- Publish prayer guidelines and study material for individuals and groups.
- Invite groups to organize prayer events – for example an overnight prayer vigil for the youth group.

- Teach about listening to God, and the different ways we can listen.
- Study the Bible.
- Observe how God is working in other churches today.

One diocese[2] suggested that on a Sunday morning the whole church could make a collage to illustrate the phrase 'The Kingdom of God is like . . .' and, using paint and material, everyone could have the chance to illustrate a piece of Scripture where Jesus speaks about or demonstrates the Kingdom of God. This could be followed up with 'God's dream for his world . . .', and 'God's dream for our neighbourhood . . .'.

Prayer flows through all phases of the MAP process – not just at the start.

Desire

In the diocese of Blackburn, Bishop Nicholas invited all churches to produce a MAP during 2006 – his second year in post. He addressed church leaders at one of the annual Visitations[3] in May, and asked that mission should become a regular PCC agenda item, as each church prayerfully works out its priorities for mission. He requested a copy of all church MAPs by the end of the year, so that he could pray for the churches and become aware of their priorities. Around 85 per cent of churches sent their MAPs to Bishop Nicholas and he was impressed by their prayerfully thought-out plans.

However, there were exceptions: one church had held its PCC meeting during June, and dutifully found space for mission on the agenda. It was decided that this was a job for the vicar, and he was asked to produce the MAP. The vicar added this to his long list of tasks; he was taking care of three village churches and there were many demands on his time. During the week before the deadline, the vicar produced a MAP document on his own and sent it off to the Bishop. The Action Plan was:

One vicar's Action Plan

1	To erect a notice board	PCC	Spring 07
2	Produce a quarterly newsletter	PCC	Spring 07
3	Research grants available to repair the hall	PCC	Spring 07
4	Complete the welcome pack (started last year)	PCC	Spring 07
5	Arrange meeting to consider monthly family service	PCC	Spring 07

Although these actions were relevant for the life of the church, one is left feeling that an opportunity was missed. Many of these are the normal business of a PCC, and there is no mention of care of people, building faith or outreach into the community. The uniform 'who' and 'when' columns indicate that the actions are not sufficiently thought through or owned. There could be many reasons for this, but the most fundamental reason was a lack of basic desire for mission work.

Antoine de Saint-Exupéry wrote: 'If you want to build a ship, don't summon people to buy wood, prepare tools, distribute jobs, and organize the work, rather teach people to yearn for the wide, boundless ocean.'[4] If we want people to produce a MAP, first, we have to teach people – especially church leaders – to yearn to respond to Jesus Christ's teachings and commandments.

The four key stages of the MAP process

In Chapter 1, we described the basic MAP process, suitable for a church new to the MAP approach. In the cycle of MAP, a church may feel that it wants to spend more time and depth in reviewing its situation, or more time to develop a Vision statement. This section describes an expanded process which is used by several dioceses in the UK. It could be used as a whole, or parts of it could be added into the basic MAP process, depending on what is relevant. However, the two pre-requisites mentioned at the beginning of this chapter remain: *prayer* and establishing *desire* for mission work.

In Chapter 5, two case examples are described, and Appendix 1 contains a practical example programme which a church might follow. Figure 5.1 shows the MAP process in diagrammatic form.

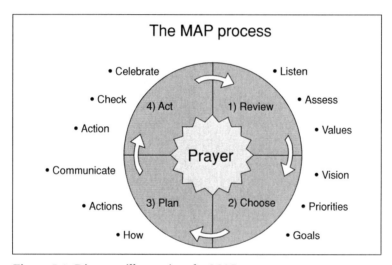

Figure 5.1 Diagram illustrating the MAP process

Phase 1   Review

In the review phase of the MAP process, a church aims to discern God's mission plan for the communities served by prayerfully looking at and understanding the situation that a church finds itself in – the location, the people, the activities that the church is engaged in and what activities could be started. There are three stages that help with this (see Figure 5.2).

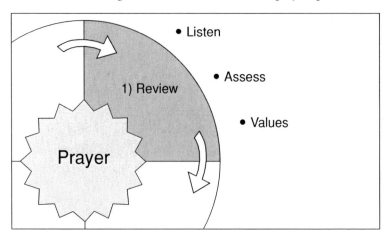

Figure 5.2 The key stages of the Review phase

(a) Listen

In the introduction to the MAP process in Chapter 1, we wrote about the 'triple listening' approach to emphasize that the church leaders should listen to at least two relevant populations: the church members and the local community, while listening to God. Church members will be involved in enacting the plan, so they should be involved in the MAP process from the beginning. If they can see how the plan is emerging, based on prayer and consultation, they are more likely to be enthusiastic about the plans and give their active support. A key part of listening to church members is to find out how the current mission actions are going – how they are perceived; how they are progressing; how they are contributing to the mission priorities. There could also be questions about what further mission needs there are.

The MAP plans should also take account of the needs of the local community, so it is important to become aware of these. A number of resources can be used to listen; for example: questionnaires, group discussions, visiting a sample of homes and places where people meet already, writing to local organizations, and so on. The listening exercises will typically find answers to questions like:

- What is the demographic of the church compared with the neighbourhood served?
- What are the demographic trends?[5]
- What are the social and pastoral needs?
- How is the church involved in the life of the community and what other opportunities are there?
- What contact points or interfaces already exist between the church and community?
- What does the community expect from the church?

Although triple listening takes time to plan, carry out and summarize, it is crucial to the process because it helps to prevent the review being only introspective, and encourages a healthy balance between mission and maintenance.

(b) Assess your strengths, weaknesses and opportunities

In this part the church conducts an assessment about how things are, what is going well, and what are the sticking points or difficulties that are encountered. This is like the church holding a mirror up to itself and taking a realistic look! It has been found very useful for church leaders to do this by using one or more of the following recommended methods, perhaps with the help of an external facilitator.

- A 'SWOT analysis' – using group discussions to agree Strengths, Weaknesses, Opportunities and Threats. This is best done by sharing feelings in a group discussion. There are many ways to do this, but a popular method is to get people into groups, then ask individuals, working on their own, to write their feelings about church strengths on Post-It! notes – one note for each strength. After about five minutes, repeat this for weaknesses, opportunities and threats.

Now each person is invited to stick these Post-It! notes on a wall or flipchart stand and explain his or her SWOT feelings to the rest of the group. Encourage the rest of the group to ask questions to clarify what is meant, but do not allow personal criticism. As this progresses, the leader or facilitator should move the notes into like groups, so that a consensus about the main SWOTs begins to emerge. At the end of the exercise, the leader summarizes the main SWOTs, and records these for later use – perhaps to share with other leaders or the church council – and to use in the next stages of the MAP process. This SWOT method takes about two hours to complete. It may be that some church leaders have encountered the SWOT method before, perhaps in their working life, and they may be able to facilitate this process for their church. It is helpful to use the SWOT method every time an annual review is conducted, both because new situations occur over time, and also so that people can see evidence of progress year on year. The SWOT may provide all that is necessary for the assessment part of the *Review phase* when used for the first time, but in subsequent years, it is recommended that one or more of the following surveys is also conducted.

- **A church health survey** – using the 'Seven Marks of a Healthy Church' published in *The Healthy Churches' Handbook*, by Robert Warren.[6] The seven marks are:

1 Energized by faith
2 Outward-looking focus
3 Seeks to find out what God wants
4 Faces the cost of change and growth
5 Operates as a community
6 Makes room for all
7 Does a few things and does them well.

Research has found that these marks are present as strengths in healthy churches that are growing. Robert Warren suggests

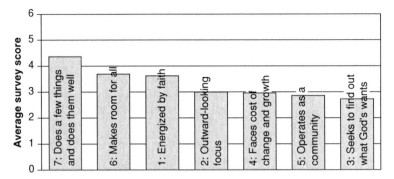

Figure 5.3 Sample 'Healthy Church' profile (St Anne's 2007)

that church leaders should discover which one or two of these are weak in their own church, and work at improving these first – because it is necessary to be healthy in all seven areas, but impossible to work on all at the same time. The book describes each of the marks and contains a questionnaire that can be used to assess the church health for each one. The results are presented back to the group, and this forms the basis of the 'Choose' section. There are very good guidelines in the book for how to conduct the assessment. As with the SWOT method, it is possible to carry out this assessment in about two hours. Figure 5.3 shows a sample. 'Healthy Church' profile.

- **A church quality survey** – using 'Natural Church Development' (NCD) by Christian Schwarz[7] and leading to an assessment of each of the 'Eight Quality Characteristics' of a healthy church. These are:

  1 Empowering leadership
  2 Gift-orientated lay ministry
  3 Passionate spirituality
  4 Functional structures
  5 Inspiring worship services
  6 Holistic small groups

7 Need-orientated evangelism
8 Loving relationships.

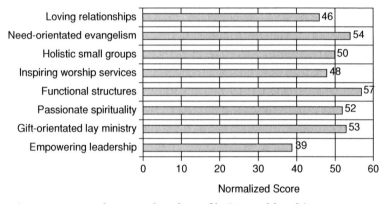

Figure 5.4 **Sample NCD church profile (St Cuthbert's)**

See Chapter 3 for more background about this approach. The assessment is carried out by using questionnaires for 30 church members, and a different one for the minister. The analysis has to be carried out by the NCD organization for a fee of about £125. They return a 'normalized profile' – one that has been adjusted for national characteristics – so that a score of 50 indicates that 50 per cent of the churches in the UK would be above and below that score. For the statistically minded, the normalized standard deviation is equivalent to a score of 15. So about 15 per cent of churches would have a score above 65, and below 35. The research has concluded that churches that have a minimum score of 65 for all the characteristics are growing in numbers.

Figure 5.4 gives a sample NCD church profile, which indicates that this church should work first on its weaker area – leadership – using the relevant parts of its stronger characteristics of structures, evangelism, lay ministry and passionate spirituality. Note: we recommend that this advanced approach is carried out with help from a trained consultant.[8]

The NCD approach is more cumbersome than the Healthy Churches approach and for some the language can be a barrier (e.g. 'biotic principles', 'the bipolar church concept'). The NCD handbook describes its own process for how to use the result of the survey, but this misses out some key stages of the MAP process. For example, there is little mention of the importance of developing a *Vision* for the church's future (see the next section – Choose). However, many churches have been helped by using the approach as a tool for discovering more about their state within the Review phase of the MAP process. We recommend the NCD approach as an assessment tool for churches that have used the SWOT and Healthy Churches approaches in previous review cycles, and are looking for new insights.

- **Other assessment methods** – A church could also consider inviting someone from the diocese/district or a neighbouring church to conduct an audit for 'Welcome', 'Worship' or 'Buildings'. Another worthwhile approach is to learn from other churches, church organizations, books, websites, etc. For example in 2006, Lichfield diocese published a booklet describing 'Ten things that make a church grow' for their churches. These were:

1 Prayer
2 Focus on health, not numbers
3 Get your church noticed!
4 Use your building
5 Model generous hospitality
6 Review your service plan
7 Help midweek groups *become* church, not a bridge to church
8 Release the gifts of children
9 Tune into today's spiritual climate
10 Rethink Christmas.

Each of these approaches leads to an assessment of strong areas and weak areas, and following this, the PCC can develop a consensus about what the opportunities are for the future. These might include working with ecumenical partners or neighbouring churches.

(c) Mission values

During the Review phase, a very useful exercise is to consider the local churches' values, and how these are reflected in current programmes, priorities and perceived behaviour. This will further prepare a church for the next phase of the MAP process – Choose – helping to make their approach sufficiently broad, and based on firm foundations. Values are defined as 'beliefs of a person or social group in which they have an emotional investment', or 'general guiding principles that govern all activities'. An understanding of church values can have a powerful effect on the motivation and desire of church members. The study of these values could include a discussion about 'to what extent are we engaged in each of these?'

If this is new to your church, you could make a start by discussing the values of the church organization that you belong to. For example, the five marks of mission of the worldwide Anglican Communion:

- To proclaim the good news of the Kingdom;
- To teach, baptize and nurture new believers;
- To respond to human need by loving service;
- To seek to transform unjust structures of society;
- To strive to safeguard the integrity of creation and sustain and renew the earth.

Or the 'Five Values for Missionary Churches' published in the report *Mission-shaped Church*, referred to in Chapter 3.[9]

- A missionary church is focused on God the Holy Trinity
  – Worship lies at its heart

- A missionary church is relational
  - Welcoming and providing hospitality; open to change
- A missionary church is incarnational
  - Shaping itself to the local culture
- A missionary church makes disciples
  - Calling people to faith; encouraging gifts; transforming individuals
- A missionary church is transformational
  - Existing for the transformation of the local church and community.

Many churches produce a 'Mission statement' to capture in a few words the purpose or values of a particular church. The statement informs people about why the church exists and what it believes in. For example: 'We are a community church – here to share the good news of Jesus Christ and to serve this community in his love.' The Mission statement should not be confused with the Vision statement – discussed in the next phase.

(d) Review completed and ongoing actions

Review how things have been progressing with previous decisions about mission plans and actions. Celebrate what has worked well and give recognition to those who have worked on them. Consider what did not work out well, and learn from this. Were resources stretched too far? Did those responsible have sufficient support? Were there sufficient reviews of progress during the last year? Was there adequate communication? Ask questions like this in order to discover what you should improve next time you identify actions – in the 'Plan' phase.

Review summary

Before moving into the Choose phase, summarize your current state – as discovered in the Review phase. The SWOT headings can be used for this summary, taking in all the learning points arrived at during the assessments also. We recommend that the summary is written in a short document, and distributed to all those who took part in the review. Ask for comments, and make any changes that are necessary to build consensus. The summary ought to be owned by all the leaders before it is communicated more widely to church members.

Phase 2   Choose

In the Choose phase, church leaders prayerfully discern how God wants to shape the church's future. This may include: how to serve the community; how to respond to peoples' needs; how to relate to other churches and how to use its resources in the best way. Figure 5.5 shows the three stages that help to get to this point.

(a) Vision

In his landmark book about the learning organization, Peter Senge cites the example of Spartacus – the story of a Roman gladiator/slave who led an army of slaves in an uprising in 71 BC.[10] They defeated the Roman legions twice, but were finally conquered by the general, Marcus Crassus, after a long siege

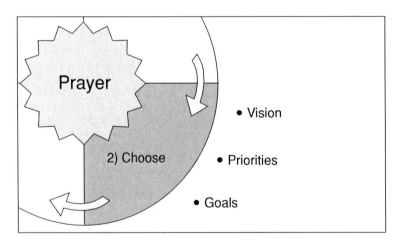

Figure 5.5 The key stages of the Choose phase

and battle. In the film, Crassus tells the thousand survivors in Spartacus's army, 'You have been slaves. You will be slaves again. But you will be spared your rightful punishment of crucifixion by the mercy of the Roman legions. All you need to do is turn over to me the slave Spartacus, because we do not know him by sight.' After a long pause, Spartacus (played by Kirk Douglas) stands up and says, 'I am Spartacus.' Then the man next to him stands up and also says, 'I am Spartacus.' The next man stands up and says, 'No, I am Spartacus.' Within a minute, everyone in the army is on his feet.

It does not matter whether this story is apocryphal or not; it demonstrates a deep truth. Each man, by standing up, chose death. But the loyalty of Spartacus's army was not to Spartacus the man. Their loyalty was to a shared vision which Spartacus had inspired: the idea that they could be free men. This vision was so compelling that no man could bear to give it up and return to slavery. Senge goes on to say that

> A shared vision is not an idea. It is not even an important idea such as freedom. It is, rather, a force in people's hearts, a force of impressive power. It may be inspired by an idea, but once it goes further – if it is compelling enough to acquire the support of more than one person – then it is no longer an abstraction. It is palpable. People begin to see it as if it exists. Few, if any, forces in human affairs are as powerful as shared vision.[11]

Secular organizations adopted the concept of vision from religious organizations. Now, we in the Church can see how they have used this concept so powerfully. In his book *Hit the Ground Kneeling*, Stephen Cottrell emphasizes how critical it is for church leaders to develop their own vision.[12] Here are some of the statements he makes:

'Vision is the mountain top; the destination we long to reach.'
'It is the vision of how things can be at the end that motivates and inspires everything else.'

'One of the primary roles of leadership is to articulate the vision of the organization.'

'The leader is the guardian and the herald of the vision.'

'The leader not only articulates the vision but also embodies it.'

'Every time the leader speaks it is a recollection of why the organization exists.'

Producing a Vision statement is a crucial part of the MAP process. The Vision statement goes beyond a Mission statement – it communicates the overall focus and aim of the church in the future, looking about five years ahead. A good Vision statement, shared and supported by people, can inspire them to pray about the future and to get involved in practical ways.

It acts like a compass and a magnet – pointing the way ahead, and drawing people to work together. It also helps each person to decide what is important for them as they go about their daily lives. The Vision statement should be brief – so that people can remember it. It needs to be shaped in prayerful consultation with the people – because to be inspired, they need to really believe in it, and take it to heart. This does not mean that the Vision statement should be produced by a committee! Rather, in practice, the key themes of the vision are developed through teaching, prayer and discussion, and finally, a small group of leaders turn this into a memorable short sentence.

The vision needs to be inspiring, but real – if the members don't really believe in the vision, then they will only do their part in the Plan out of obedience or loyalty, and probably the Plan will not be effective. It is better to have a more limited vision that most people are 'on board' with, than an ambitious vision that no one much believes in. Example: 'We will become a growing church where all ages can grow in faith and receive spiritual support, and with a reputation for loving service to the local community.' See Appendix 1 for ideas about producing a vision.

(b) Priorities

If you have a good Vision statement, the priorities will natural-ly flow from it. The main difficulty comes when you have to balance ambition with practical resources. The word priority, which means 'the greatest importance: the state of having most importance or urgency', has been used deliberately in the MAP process because experience has shown that it is not possible to work on too many strategic initiatives at the same time. MAPs that contain ten priority areas for action will most likely lead to disappointment. The chosen priorities may be new things that have not been done before, or they may be things that are already being done but need building or expanding. At this stage, a 'priority' is not yet a fully developed SMART goal, as will be described in the next section – it is simply a statement of a *desired state*. Examples:

- 'To be continuously running Emmaus courses for various groups, so that people can find ways to grow as disciples.'
- 'To start a Fresh Expression for mothers and toddlers.'

Priorities can be long term or short term, so it is best to arrive at priorities in two steps. First, consider what are the priorities for reaching your vision. Then second, for each priority con-sider the next 12 months – what can the church work on from a practical point of view. From experience, the ideal number of strategic priorities for an average-sized church for any one year is two or three. No church should choose more than five. Is your church trying to do too much this year?

(c) Goals

Churches have discovered that in order to bring each priority to life, the priority needs to be translated into a goal state-ment. These are written in such a way that everyone will know what is to be achieved. To do this in the best way, we use the

SMART method to arrive at the goals. The aim is to make each goal:

Specific: Being clear about what is the goal and who it is aimed at – example: 'engage with young adults aged 18–30'.

Measurable: Being clear about what is the overall target and how progress will be measured and assessed. It is very important to choose the right thing to measure! As a rule of thumb, try to measure the outcome that is desired, but if this is not possible or too difficult, select the most appropriate leading indicator – examples: 'to see an increase in total attendance of the 18–30 age group of 10 per cent'; 'to establish four home groups'.

Achievable: Ensuring that people believe that the goal is significant, but possible.

Resourced: Ensuring that there are sufficient human and financial resources.

Timed: Being clear about the timing for completing the goal – examples: 'by the end of May'; 'within the next year'.

So an example of a goal statement could be: 'To engage more with young adults aged 18 to 30 so that we see an increase in Sunday and midweek regular attendance of 10 per cent within 12 months.'

Each goal is likely to have a large number of actions associated with it (see next section), so it is good practice to appoint an 'owner' who takes overall responsibility for co-ordinating the work. The owner could be the vicar/minister, but if not, the owner should keep in close contact with him/her and the PCC/council, who have overall responsibility for the MAP.

Finally, not all the goals will be new ones; some will be ongoing work. However, it is always useful to affirm these goals in the new plan, and there is the opportunity to revise wording and timing as necessary.

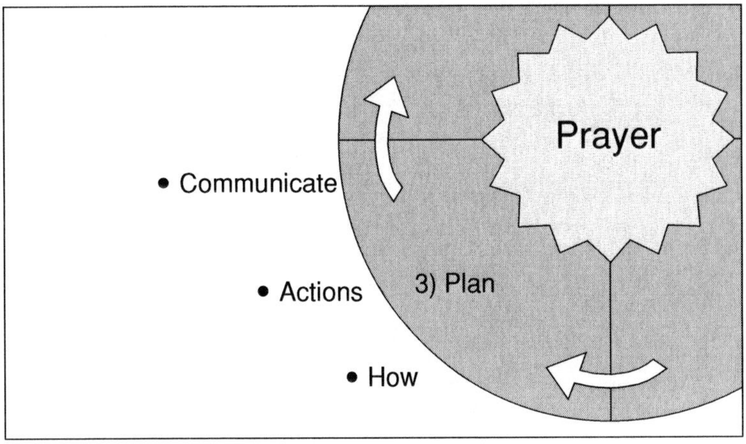

Figure 5.6 The key stages of the Plan phase

Phase 3   Plan

The key stages of the Plan phase are shown in Figure 5.6.

(a) How

The first part of the third phase – planning – is to take each priority goal one by one and to consider how it will be achieved. Start by using words to describe all the various conditions, training, resources, purchases or other items or factors that need to be in place before the goal can be achieved. Some groups approach this by using the 'When' method to identify the key actions and milestones. For example, if the goal is to attract more young families to the church, the PCC/council could write the following statement on a blank wall or piece of paper, and arrive at a list of conditions: 'We will attract more young families to this church when . . .'. A number of suggestions will be made, and you can take each one, and break it down into a series of further 'when's, and build up a kind of tree structure (see Figure 5.7). This will help you to arrive at the required actions in the next section.

We will attract more young families
to church WHEN

- We start a toddler group
  - We find a leader
  - We decorate the hall
  - We recruit helpers
  - We write policy and procedures
  - We advertise
  - We talk to baptism families
- We have monthly family services
  - We have more modern worship songs
  - We have a kid's worship leader
  - We find a suitable liturgy
  - We have more lay leaders
- We improve our welcome
  - We train sides-persons
  - We create a welcome pack
  - We decorate the porch
  - We improve the entrance lighting
- We get advice from others
  - We invite the children's advisor to speak to the PCC
  - We visit All Saints and St Anne's

Figure 5.7 The 'When' method to identify and structure Plans

(b) Actions

There may be several levels of actions for each goal, because each main action can usually be broken down into further detail. However, for the MAP summary, a church should only list the top-level actions – otherwise there is a danger of becoming lost in the detail! It helps a great deal if the 'How' section above has been done, because all the various 'Hows' and/or 'Whens' can be considered and, usually, there is a logical way to group them together under similar headings. When the main actions have been defined, the next step is to identify owners and timing. In practice, it is useful to record actions on paper with the following column headings:

WHAT: defining the precise action to be done.
WHEN: the target date for completion.
WHO: identifying who is responsible for the action.

At the end of the planning phase, check that the total plan has integrity with regard to content, timing and resource. The key questions are:

1 Looking at the WHAT column, will all the actions associated with a particular priority goal really deliver that goal?
2 Looking at the WHEN column, will the goals which depend on relevant actions be completed within the planned time in the right sequence?
3 Looking at the WHO column, add up how much work each named individual is taking on – can they all cope? Is the vicar/minister overloaded?

Finally, consider whether there are any training needs for each individual, and if so, produce a training plan.

(c) Communicate

It may be that many people have been involved in contributing to the MAP process, but even so, the final MAP summary needs to be widely communicated. This should be short enough to be read and understood by everyone, and detailed enough to avoid misunderstandings – two or three sides of A4 are usually enough. See Appendix 2 for example MAP summary templates. These reports can also be made available at the back of church for anyone who wants one.

There is strong evidence that a church also needs to drip-drip the Vision and the Plan through all the means of communication the church has, using such channels as:

- Themes chosen for teaching and/or for home groups
- Verbal notices in services

- The church magazine
- References in sermons
- The weekly notice sheet
- Helpful books on a church bookstall.

Communication is not a one-off event, and despite all the above, many people will only begin to get the message when they see the MAP worked out in the daily life of the church.

Phase 4   Act

The key stages in the Act phase are illustrated by Figure 5.8.

(a) Action

Now for the action! Some new actions will be started, some existing actions will continue, and some may be modified or ended. The owners of the goals and actions will often appoint teams of people to work with them and so it is important to plan times to meet for prayer, encouragement and review of progress. It is essential that the plan is kept alive, and that the actions are progressing as planned where possible. If not, the

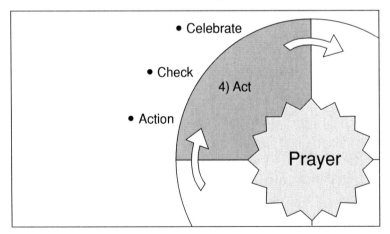

Figure 5.8 The key stages in the Act phase

plan should be modified to reflect the reality of the situation. The MAP should be a living document.

(b) Check

Here, 'check' means standing back regularly to review how things are going. Teams that are working on one action or priority must take time – preferably every month – to review progress, and make any necessary adjustments. The church leaders should also review the overall progress of all actions – every one or two months. This is not only to inform council and team members about progress, but also to provide an opportunity for them and others to contribute with further suggestions – especially if things are not going as well as expected. The MAP progress should be communicated to all church members regularly, and leaders should listen to how people react. Wall or free-standing display boards can be used to show news of what is happening; but these must be kept up to date! For goals which generate many actions, consider using a tree structure to report activities or to show the progress of the main and related measurements.

Checking, discussing and adjusting are part of the learning cycle of life, and this applies very much to the MAP activities.

(c) Celebrate

Give thanks to God when goals have been achieved or when significant milestones have been reached successfully, and celebrate! Also, it is important to recognize and give thanks for the contribution of the people involved, especially when actions have taken a lot of effort.

The MAP process as a learning cycle

A key aspect of the MAP process is its cyclical nature, and its similarity to the so called Action–Reflection learning cycle (see Figure 5.9). The Act phase leads into a review phase when it is

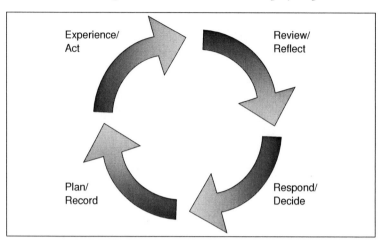

Figure 5.9 The Action–Reflection learning/theological cycle

time to update the overall plan. For each individual church, this means that each time the cycle is repeated, a review and assessment of the state of its activities is prayerfully conducted, and the Mission and Vision statements are revised as necessary. In the Choose phase, the five-year priorities are revisited, and the new one-year priorities and actions are developed and planned. The Review and Choose phases may take one or two months to work through, and in the meantime, current actions from the previous plan continue. This cyclical approach brings several benefits:

- The action plan is refreshed and always up to date.
- The short-term issues of the church are balanced with the long-term strategy on a continuous basis.
- Church leaders develop strategic planning skills and learn more during each cycle.

The period of the cycle

The period of the overall cycle may depend on local and diocesan/area policy. Some dioceses, for example Blackburn, encourage churches to renew their MAP every year, using a five-year planning horizon. This is sometimes called a 'rolling five-year' approach. Some churches have chosen to do a very thorough process in year one, when the five-year vision and priorities are agreed, and for the next one or two years, a shorter annual review has been done to set one-year priorities and plan goals and actions. This is fine, especially if the annual review work has started with a reminder of the overall MAP process.

The annual cycle brings the advantages mentioned in the previous section plus some others:

- The Mission and Vision statements are living, and communicated effectively by the church leaders.
- The assessment stage within the Review phase can be developed year on year. For example, in the first year, a SWOT analysis may be conducted together with a congregational questionnaire; in the second year, a 'healthy churches' survey may be done, together with a community survey; in the third year, a repeat survey could be done to look into what has changed, and a survey of community groups could be conducted; and so on, so that the assessment is up to date and relevant, as the understanding of how the church really is increases.
- A yearly cycle provides positive learning experiences for strategic planning skills. If the cycle is longer, some aspects may be forgotten, and have to be relearned.

However, it is for each church to decide on the most appropriate period. MAP work should be joyful and not onerous. It should be fresh and not stale from overworking.

A 10-point health check for your MAP

After completing a MAP, or before starting the Review phase of the next MAP, it may be useful to do a health check. The following checklist is based on the key stages of the MAP process; however, a church may decide to adapt this to its own circumstances. Here is a 10-point checklist.

1 **Rooted in** *prayer*
   - Has the whole MAP process been rooted in prayer – at every stage?
   - Has a whole-church prayer event been organized to discern God's calling for the church?
   - Have there been other pauses to listen to God at various stages?
   - Have relevant prayers been distributed to church members for personal prayer?

2 *Listen*: **consulting those impacted by the MAP**
   - Has a community audit been conducted?
   - Have key community leaders (for example other church leaders, police, business, council, and so on) been interviewed to find out what they think about community needs and how the church might serve the area?
   - Have a sample of the non-church community residents been interviewed to discover their views about the church?
   - Have church members been consulted to discover their thoughts and ideas about how the church might develop in future?

3 *Assess*: **taking a close look at your church**
   - As part of the assessment stage, has at least one of the following assessments been conducted by the church council:
     - A SWOT analysis?
     - A Healthy Church survey?
     - A NCD survey?
   - Have diocesan resources and/or other churches been approached to help with your assessment or to give you ideas for how to assess your state?

- Have you considered a supplementary audit, for example:
  - A welcome audit?
  - A worship audit?
  - A buildings audit?

4 *Values*: **being clear about the church's main purposes and sources of energy**
  - Have the church values been published?
  - Is there a good, well thought out Mission statement which is owned by the church council?
  - Is there a sense that the church council members look to God for inspiration, energy and direction?

5 *Vision*: **being clear about the future direction**
  - Is there a good, well thought out five-year Vision statement?
    - Has it arisen after wide consultation?
    - Is the Vision statement being frequently communicated?
    - Is it owned by the church council?
    - Is the Vision statement really shared by all?
    - Does it paint a clear picture of the long-term future (about five years ahead)?
    - Does it inspire commitment and motivation?
    - Can church members memorize it?

6 *Priorities*: **the vital ingredients to deliver the vision**
  - Has the church council identified the key priorities from an understanding of the Vision statement?
    - Have longer-term priorities been broken down into priorities for the next year?
    - Are there a manageable number of priorities?
    - Do they sufficiently describe a desired state?
  - Has the church council made choices about what not to do?
    - Have some activities been stopped or put on hold in order to resource the priorities?

7 *Goals*: **being smart with priorities**
  - Have annual SMART goals been identified for each annual priority?
  - Has an owner been identified for each goal (the individual who will be responsible for actions)?
  - Can all the goals be achieved with the available resources and funding?

8 *Actions*: **planning to succeed**
  - Have the necessary actions for each goal been identified?
  - Has each action been defined in terms of WHAT, WHEN and WHO?
  - Has an overall resource check been done (to ensure that no one is over-committed)?

9 *Communication*: **keeping everyone informed**
  - Has the MAP been summarized and communicated?
    - Does this include a summary of the Review and Assessment phases as well as the Choose phase?
  - Have all appropriate vehicles been used for communication?
    - Notices, magazine, preaching, notice board . . .
    - Are spare copies available for people to pick up in church or at meetings?
  - Do people have the opportunity to ask questions to aid understanding?
  - Is there a plan for reinforcing the communication?

10 *Checking Progress*: **keeping control of the overall plan**
  - Is the overall progress regularly reviewed in church council meetings?
  - Are the plans updated and amended when necessary?
  - Are the plans adapted to cope with new circumstances?
  - Do the owners of each priority meet with all those who are responsible for actions associated with their priority?
  - Are completed actions celebrated?
  - Are the efforts of those involved sufficiently recognized?

6

Case examples

---•·◆·•---

St Anne, Fence-in-Pendle

REPORTED BY MIKE CHEW

Fence-in-Pendle is a rural village on the outskirts of Burnley in Lancashire. There are many towns and villages like this in the Blackburn diocese, and St Anne's Church is a 'middle of the road' church with average attendance: 75 adults and 15 children. They produced their first MAP in 2005 in response to the request from the Bishop. In late 2007, they had worked through most of the actions, and now wanted to produce a new plan based on a long-term strategy. Richard Adams, the vicar, asked me to facilitate the process, so I met with him to work out a suitable programme for an away-day. Richard is a busy priest who also leads another church in a neighbouring village. Nevertheless, he'd found the first MAP very useful, and now wanted to go through the MAP process with more thoroughness.

The Fence PCC had gone through a SWOT analysis in the first MAP, and had also revised their Mission statement. Many actions had been listed, and most of these had been completed. During the meeting with Richard, we concluded that it would be useful to go through a 'healthy churches' survey, and to develop a Vision statement. Also, Richard wanted the PCC to regard the MAP process as a spiritual journey, so the programme for the day needed to reflect this. A local Christian conference centre was booked for a Saturday 9 a.m. to 4 p.m., two months ahead to give the PCC enough notice. At the conclusion of the meeting with Richard, we knew what we wanted to get out of the day, but we decided not to produce a detailed programme for the day, as we didn't want to constrain the working of the Holy Spirit.

The day went well – Richard and the PCC members were pleased with the outcome, and the two worship sessions – morning prayer and a final Eucharist – were appreciated. We are grateful to Richard for giving us permission to reproduce below the PCC's working papers, and the MAP.

Review Phase

A. Review of the status of previous Actions and Priorities

We have reviewed and reflected on our main actions from 2005/6, as follows.

1. Run an Emmaus Prayer course.
This was done: 53 people were invited and 14 responded positively. The course ran in two groups, led by a mixture of experienced and new leaders. Feedback was positive and fruit in individual lives can still be seen growing.

2. Serve coffee in foyer rather than hall.
The purpose was to draw new people who are on the edge of the fellowship into the beginnings of friendships with established church members. There have been all sorts of logistical and safety issues with coffee in the foyer, but a system which works has been developed and we now do this once a month, on family service Sunday (see 4 below). These changes, along with the changing congregation at family services, have led to some experimental furniture rearrangements under an archdeacon's faculty.

3. Offer short courses, 2 or 3 times per year, on basics of faith & living.
We have not achieved this in terms of frequency, but have run two "Start!" (CPAS) courses and one "Life Balance"

(Robert Warren & Susan Mayfield) course. All have been highly valued by those attending.

4. Modify 'family service' liturgy to be more accessible to unchurched young people.
A family service team was appointed by the PCC to develop and lead a Service of the Word, with mainly lay leadership and focused on participation and involvement of children. This was done for a 6 month experimental period, inviting past contacts from baptisms and weddings. Attendance has been high, and some people have started coming to other services. After the experimental period, the service has been made a permanent monthly feature.

5. Develop prayer helpline and website "sayoneforme.org".
No progress made: people to take the idea onward have not been found.

6. Corporate prayer: offering a variety of opportunities and encouragements has met with little or no response.

7. Integrating newcomers: progress is being made, including drawing one new person onto the family service leadership team. The established congregation in general is not taking initiatives with newcomers, mainly leaving it to PCC members. Teaching has been given, but more needs to be done on creating a culture of welcome.

8. Hospitality: some individuals are working hard on this, and during this year new social networking occasions have been set up. Still work to do . . .

B. Assessment

Healthy Churches Survey

(Using 'Seven Marks of a Healthy Church')

[See Figure 5.3 on p. 63.]

SWOT Summary – *updated during our review, with the help of the survey.*

Strengths
- Welcome
- Inclusiveness
- Doing a few things well
- Music at Sunday services

Weaknesses
- Corporate prayer
- Befriending and integration of newcomers
- Relevant teaching about growth (Personal and corporate)

Opportunities
- The Alpha course (shared with the 2 other churches in Fence)
- Wide range of visitors, especially via baptisms, marriages and uniformed organizations' services

C. Mission Statement

We reviewed our mission statement and decided not to change it:

"We, God's people in the parish of St. Anne, Fence, Burnley, in dependence on the Holy Spirit, seek to:

- *worship God with sincerity of heart;*
- *share the good news of the Gospel of Jesus Christ;*
- *have fellowship with all our brothers and sisters in Christ;*
- *offer welcome and service to all people in this community;*
- *witness to Christian values in our personal and corporate lives."*

D. Values

- Meeting needs (what needs do we see here in this community?)
- Answers to life (what are the big questions?)
- Drawing people to God (how can we best do this?)
- Adapt (how should we do this?)
- Making a difference

Choose Phase

A. *Vision Statement*

We formulated a new vision statement:

> *"St. Anne's: providing opportunities for everyone to develop their Christian faith while reaching out locally and beyond."*

B. *Priorities for 2008*

1 Prayer & worship
2 Local community mission
3 Social
4 Mission beyond the locality
5 Teaching & learning

Plan Phase

A. *Initial Actions Agreed*

1. Prayer & Worship
Find out needs & plan prayer & worship opportunities
Parents & children events (involve older people)
Older people – lunch club? link with village hall events?
Overcoming initial prayer barriers

- Fortnightly food & prayer (Connie Clark)
- Home communion groups (Connie Clark)

2. Local Community Mission
Supporting Fence Village Hall (FVH) initiatives. Network to link FVH, the churches, school to ensure mutual support and coordination. (Pam Barton, Rosemary Hartley, Dawn McFadyen)

3. Social
A programme across the year to ensure that there is something on each month to help us share time together and invite friends: integrate with FVH and other churches' events. (Becky Joseph, Gail Smith, Dawn McFadyen)

4. Mission beyond local
Uganda works well – keep doing it!
"Middle-distance gap" exists

Congregation survey – who's involved with what at the moment?
Diocesan Board for Social Responsibility – neighbours but not much contact (Simon Parker)

5. Teaching & Learning
Courses: (Richard Adams)

- After Alpha?
- Other enquiry & initiation courses e.g. Start, Emmaus nurture etc.
- Emmaus growth courses – survey to discover congregational interest

Website resources for prayer & study (Andrew Stringer)

B. Evaluation process

We recognise a need to incorporate regular evaluation and review of everything we do (Andrew Stringer, Richard Adams & Simon Parker to devise an approach)

C. Communication

We need to present this to the whole church, and agreed on this format:

Sunday 22nd June

- Sermon slot to comprise an overview plus two minutes from each lead person above, describing their action area and indicating help needed.
- Handout (a shortened version of this document) to be given out on that day.
- Each lead person to prepare a simple display outlining their area and help needed, these to be put on display boards on 22nd June and left up for a month for people to see and think about.
- After 4 weeks, a lunch or cake 'n coffee after a couple of Sunday services to ask people to commit to an action area.

Comment and observations

As I was writing about this case example, I interviewed Richard Adams and invited him to reflect on what differences MAP had brought to the church and himself. He felt that:

- MAP has enabled them to review everything they do from a mission perspective and this has led to several positive changes.
- MAP has helped the church to take new initiatives to reach children and young families in a better way.
- MAP has given the PCC the authority and resources to take a lead in planning mission activities.
- MAP has provided a focus on the future, and a process for working out mission strategy, which would not have been done as well without it.
- MAP has taught them the value of self-evaluation.
- The diocesan Mission statement emphasis on 'Growing up Growing out' has been the catalyst for reaching out more into the community, with some resulting fruit, and has led some people to become more committed disciples – especially those in leadership positions. Also, some people who used to be on the 'fringe' have moved to be 'outer core'.
- The MAP summary document has provided a useful framework for the annual report.

I invited Richard to comment on the use of the MAP process. He said that the PCC had found the work on the Vision statement tough – it was hard to come up with a short and punchy statement, which was sufficiently future-focused. For himself, he was used to having 'mini-visions' in his head for specific aspects of church life, but articulating a whole church vision was difficult. However, having worked out the new Vision statement, he is finding it very useful, especially when discussing priorities. When reviewing new and existing ideas and tasks, the PCC are now used to the question, 'Is this part of our vision?'

I also asked Richard about the time period for the MAP process – noting that the second MAP had been completed two years after the first MAP. He felt that an annual review of priorities, goals and actions by the PCC was appropriate, but that two years was about right for the health assessment (SWOT or survey) and a major review of the Mission and Vision statements, given that they are a small church with lots of activity but with a shared vicar and no other paid staff. Furthermore, slavish adherence to a fixed timetable isn't always possible or healthy: when experiments are being carried out, the results can't be predicted, nor can the time they'll take to work into a church's life.

All Saints Wellington with Eyton

MARK IRELAND

All Saints is the parish church of Wellington, Shropshire (population of parish: 14,000), a formerly independent market town which is now part of the Telford new town conurbation. The parish has a long history (with a resident priest recorded in the Domesday Book), a strong evangelical tradition and a congregation with an average Sunday attendance (when I arrived) of 163 adults and 40 children. There is also a small district church within the parish, serving the tiny farming hamlet of Eyton (population: 30). It was my privilege to succeed Prebendary Malcolm Potter, whose distinguished 20-year ministry had seen significant growth in numbers and in faith, the development of local lay ministry and the re-ordering of the church building.

All Saints is a parish with a long history of Mission Action Planning, based on a five-year cycle. When I arrived as vicar in January 2007, the parish was well into the implementation of its strategic vision *Towards 2010*, which had been adopted in 2005 after a long process of prayer, study, review and consultation among the congregation. Fortunately, I was already familiar with some of the recent history of the parish, having been used by the previous incumbent as an outside consultant in reviews of both its local ministry scheme and its Mission Action Plan.

However, while it was very exciting to become part of a parish with a well-developed mission agenda, it was also daunting to be faced with a very full pre-set agenda for the early years of one's incumbency, with over one hundred specific goals set out in the documentation. Simply implementing the already overcrowded agenda would have left me with no space to bring my own gifts and insights to the mix. The challenge I faced was how to honour the work which had gone into producing the parish's MAP while also creating space for the new incumbent to be (in the words of the parish profile) 'an innovator, willing to take risks for God, taking initiatives to discover and implement God's vision for the future'.

I talked this over with Canon Robert Warren, in his role as larger churches consultant to the diocese. We floated the idea of doing some kind of congregation-wide consultation to refocus the vision and direction in the light of my arrival, but quickly realized that there was little appetite for another large-scale consultation so soon after the last one. Instead, having spent considerable time praying and reflecting on both the existing MAP, the parish's 'statement of need' (drawn up to send to prospective incumbents), my own observations and my discussions with the Bishop and leaders within the parish during the appointment process, I simply outlined at my first PCC meeting (in January 2007) five priorities for my first year, which were:

Priorities identified at PCC in January 2007

1 Growing in our relationship with God
2 Growing out in fresh expressions of church, and in the community
3 Growing together with St Catherine's
4 Releasing new ministries
5 Reaching out in mission beyond the parish

These were well received, and were simply overlaid on the existing MAP. A few months later, at my first annual meeting, the deputy leader of the ministry team showed the PowerPoint of the original MAP *Towards 2010* and commented on how far on the parish was with implementing the various goals. I then outlined the five priorities for my first year which I had discussed with the PCC, which then became part of the revised MAP. These were then worked on with the PCC and ministry team over the coming 12 months.

At the end of my first year I reviewed our progress with the PCC and picked up from the meeting much excitement about the many new initiatives we had introduced, but also some real anxiety about the need to pace ourselves and allow time and space for new initiatives and ideas to bed in. This led to just four priorities for my second year, the first two of which were consolidation (of new initiatives) and integration (of the new members who had joined in the last year).

At my second annual meeting my colleague repeated the slides outlining the first year's five priorities and reviewed how far we had got with each of them, before I then outlined the four priorities for the coming year. They were:

Priorities for 2008–09

- Consolidating new initiatives
- Integrating new members
- Growing the number of children and young people attending
- Giving the church hall a makeover

Midway through my second year in the parish (2008), we began to plan for a stewardship renewal process in October. We had a lively discussion in Finance Committee about whether we should wait to see what was pledged by church members in terms of planned giving, and devise our budget and plans in the light of this. I resisted this on the grounds that we should not allow our vision to be dictated by finance, and that people's willingness to give is directly related to the extent to which they are inspired by the church's vision and direction. It was clear to me, therefore, that before inviting people to commit themselves financially we had to set out a very clear vision and direction, and that for this vision to be owned by the congregation they needed a fresh opportunity to contribute their thoughts and ideas to the reworking of the medium-term vision.

Having learnt from my co-author Mike Chew about the value of devising a 'Vision statement', to express in a short and memorable sentence where a business or organization wants to be in five years' time, I felt this would be a really helpful thing for All Saints to develop, to sit alongside the long-held 'Mission statement', which expresses the church's purpose. The aim of the Vision statement is to act as a compass and a magnet, setting the direction of travel and drawing people together around a common vision and direction.

The next challenge was to design a process to enable as many of the congregation as possible to contribute, without tying up scores of people in meetings or (even worse in a family-friendly church) asking them to give up a precious Saturday for a day away. Having discussed this again with Canon Robert Warren, we came up with a really helpful model which involved people in existing gatherings, rather than creating additional meetings. I began by introducing the subject of developing a Vision statement at an evening service – to which all our cell group leaders were specifically invited, together with those who weren't in a cell group but wanted to have a chance to contribute to the vision process. At the service I began by asking all those present to write down on a slip of paper four words or phrases in answer to the question, 'If all *your* prayers were answered, what would All Saints be like in five years' time?'

If *your* prayers were answered, what would All Saints be like in 2013?

- Open
- Community
- Well-known, with a good reputation
- Going out
- Growing/full/ overflowing
- More services
- Spirit led
- Children and young people
- Deeper discipleship
- Creative hub
- Caring

Having filled in their slips, I then asked the congregation to reflect briefly on the question, 'If all *Jesus'* prayers were answered, what would All Saints be like in five years' time?' A number of common themes emerged.

After people had discussed their answers to the question, I then outlined (and explained with PowerPoint) the four words or phrases which I had chosen before the service to express where I sensed God wanted us to be as a church in five years' time. Each of our 15 cell groups was then asked at their next meeting to study the draft vision outlined and to feed back their thoughts and comments by email, with the promise that all the responses from the cells, along with any individual responses, would be displayed in church for all to see.

What was striking when we got to study all the slips handed in at the service was the very high degree of overlap and common vision between what the congregation were thinking and what I had prepared. This was an encouraging sign that the Holy Spirit was at work. When the responses came back from the cell groups, there was again a strong degree of agreement with the draft Vision statement, but a couple of key amendments were suggested which were later agreed by the PCC. These were to include the words 'in the community' and to include 'growing leaders' rather than 'training leaders'. The revised Vision statement was then approved by the PCC and unpacked in a Sunday morning sermon and in a leaflet which accompanied the giving renewal pledge form given to every church member.

All Saints Wellington Vision Statement

Jesus is calling us to become
a church known in
the community for open
doors, acts of grace, Spirit-led
worship and growing leaders

This process seemed to work well, and to be well received – as was seen in a definite increase in pledged giving at the very time when the global financial crisis was just unfolding. I am sure that in a larger church like All Saints people join us or commit to us because they are attracted by the church's vision, much more than because of a personal or pastoral relationship with a particular vicar or minister. However, the process of discerning God's vision has to be an ongoing two-way listening process, listening to God in prayer, and listening to the membership. I have discovered over the years that when God has something important for the church to hear, he is just as willing to reveal that through a quiet prayerful person in the pew – or even through the irritating person who may wind me up in a meeting – as he is through me!

Interestingly, there was one cell group whose response stood out from the others and seemed to flag up significant reservations both about the vision and the process. I therefore asked if I could attend a subsequent meeting of the group, which enabled me to hear what they were saying. The simple process of going out of my way to listen to the group seemed of itself to reassure them and bring them on board, as well as clearing up some important misunderstandings.

In March 2009 the PCC considered what should be our priorities for the coming year in the light of our five-year Vision statement. After three years of growth we have now reached the size we were 15 years ago, before the church hit a glass ceiling in the early 1990s. The PCC agreed that we should focus on just three things which we believe are vital to breaking through that glass ceiling:

1 To redevelop the parish hall, with the support of the whole church, to fulfil our Vision statement; to oversee the process, minimize disruption and secure funding.
2 To improve the operational management and administration of All Saints, to ensure we fulfil our Vision statement and support the future growth of the church.
3 To develop a varied pattern of services to ensure we fulfil our Vision statement and enable more people to worship God.

After presenting these aims for discussion at the annual meeting, the PCC and ministry team set aside a joint Saturday morning to work in groups on these three priorities. The facilitator of each group was to start with the useful sentence 'We will achieve this when we . . .' to list the actions which would be needed to fulfil the goal. Having agreed the key actions, each group would then attempt to put a named person against each action and a timescale, before presenting their work to the whole gathering for discussion. The reports from the groups were then to be written up in the light of that discussion before being submitted to the PCC for formal approval at a later date.

Work on our church's MAP continues as I write, as our MAP slowly evolves from a list of goals produced once every five years into a working document which is regularly updated at PCC, expressing both our immediate priorities for the coming year and our five-year horizon of where we sense God is leading us as a church. This rolling horizon is reflected in its new title – instead of *Towards 2010*, it is now called *Towards God's Future*.

7

MAP as part of a diocesan growth strategy

How dioceses have used MAP

In this chapter, we will look at how several dioceses have introduced MAP, their main features and what happened in the following years, especially relating to attendance trends. Interestingly, 11 out of the 19 English dioceses that we know are engaged in MAP or growth strategy initiatives (listed in Table 1.1 in Chapter 1) showed numerical growth in average weekly attendance in the years 2006 and/or 2007. This compares with 9 further dioceses showing growth out of the remaining 24.

It should be noted that we do not see growth in attendance numbers as the main goal of a growth strategy. Rather, it is the growth in mission-related areas – for example in faith, in discipleship, in worship and in spreading God's love into communities. However, if growth is taking place in these areas in a church, then growth in attendance will normally follow some time later. Clearly, an individual church may have particular issues which inhibit growth in numbers, but, on average, for a group of churches in a district, area, deanery or diocese, numerical growth should be observed.

We begin with a summary of London diocese, completing the story we started at the beginning of the book.

London 1993

In Chapter 1 we described how MAP was introduced into the London diocese. The initiative had a number of identifiable characteristics, summarized below.

Summary of main characteristics

- Bishop's initiative.
- Refocusing the diocese on mission.
- Top-down themes.
- Five-year plan for the church.
- Church MAPs to be sent to Bishop.
- Light touch for feedback from Bishop.
- Two people in MAP team to support Bishop.
- Support available on request.
- 70 per cent response from churches.
- Growth apparent as a result.

Evidence for growth

In Chapter 1, we mentioned that David Hope said he believed that Mission Action Planning contributed significantly to reversing the downward attendance spiral in the diocese – he said: 'It wouldn't have happened without MAP.' Bob Jackson has researched the reasons for the growth in membership and attendance in those years[1] and as he has written in his books,[2] that he can find no hard evidence that the MAP initiative was instrumental in the growth observed, when comparing attendance statistics for churches that sent their MAPs to the Bishop with those that did not. However, this was based on a very small number of churches in one area. On the other hand, at a recent conference in York diocese, he produced material which supports the view that the MAP initiative was one of the strategies which enabled growth to take place in London diocese. Certainly, MAP was not the only nor the instrumental activity, but he now includes MAP as one of the factors enabling the growth observed. So how do we explain these apparently conflicting conclusions?

All will be revealed later in this chapter, but for now let us consider how churches respond to a diocesan MAP initiative, and group churches into four broad categories:

Category 1: churches that fully understand the message behind the diocesan MAP/growth initiative, who become fully engaged in the process, and send their MAPs to the Bishop/diocese.

Category 2: churches that fully understood the message behind the diocesan MAP/growth initiative, who were already fully engaged in the process, but decide *not* to send their MAPs to the Bishop/diocese.

Category 3: churches that responded to the diocesan initiative, but in an impassive, mechanistic way. They send in their MAP, but it is not taken into the life of the church.

Category 4: churches that are not engaged in mission work, and decide not to respond.

With this in mind, the answer to the question: 'Does MAP produce growth in membership and attendance?'[3] becomes complicated. Comparing growth results for churches who have returned MAPs (Categories 1 and 3) with those who have not (Categories 2 and 4) – as in Bob Jackson's initial research – might well produce a result which indicates no difference in growth, because both these groups may include churches that are growing rapidly, and those that are not. To answer the question, we need to find a way to compare those churches that are using a good process for mission planning with those who are not. We come back to this later in the chapter, during the York and Blackburn stories

Our current source in London diocese – Neil Evans[4] – also supports the view that MAP has had a positive influence on growth. He believes that MAP is now in the DNA of the growing churches in the diocese. He makes this simple distinction between churches: those who take in the MAP approach and use it organically to grow their mission work, and those who use MAP as a prescriptive tool, with no spiritual dimension. He has no doubt that comparing these two groups of churches would demonstrate that MAP has had a very positive impact.

He believes that the important factor is not whether or not churches use the MAP process as suggested in diocesan guidelines, but rather whether they are engaged in a process of planning, vision-building and review – which may or may not be called MAP – and whether this is part of the life of the parish. He gets concerned with a parish which returns a MAP which looks like a box-ticking exercise, but always delights with a bright and original document or process which shows real vision and SMART goals. He commented that when discussing the MAP process with a parish he always emphasizes that the MAP process:

- should have wide ownership – both within and ideally outside the congregation;
- is a process not an event – it's not about producing a piece of paper;
- could take anything up to a year to complete, with parish and community audits;
- is an evangelistic/mission exercise, in that it should draw people in;
- is for the parish, not for the bishop (though he always gets a copy);
- is out of date the moment the ink is dry, as it should be a living, organic document;
- is not constraining, but life-giving;
- should appear in some shape or form on every PCC agenda – a litmus test as to whether it is alive or dead.

The authors fully concur with these views – as we will summarize later.

York 2000

MAP was introduced in York shortly after David Hope became Archbishop. However, it was not all plain sailing; he explained:

> There was quite a tussle to begin with about getting an agreed Mission statement for the diocese. Unlike London, which had been struggling on its beam ends, York diocese was in a better place and less convinced about the need for MAP.

He started a discussion about mission priorities in the senior team, and from that the initiative 'Living the Gospel' was started. A new Mission statement for the diocese eventually emerged, and was included in a booklet which took *Living the Gospel* as its title:

Living the Gospel

A Mission Statement for the Diocese of York

We are called by Jesus Christ to announce God's Kingdom and to make disciples.

In response, we will endeavour to:

- inspire and resource the mission of the Church and the ministry of laity and clergy
- work in co-operation with Christians of other traditions.

We commit ourselves to:

- *Attending* to God in worship, prayer, and the study of the Scriptures.
- *Exploring* the faith and its implications and challenges for life today, through teaching learning, and nurture.
- *Growing* as communities of faith, hope and love, as a sign of God's Kingdom.
- *Engaging* with God's world and its peoples, in compassion, service and evangelism.

In launching the first phase of 'Living the Gospel', David Hope recorded a 10-minute audio tape, which was sent out to each church in October 2000, with the request that it be played at a main service as soon as possible. Accompanying leaflets were sent to every church member. Archdeaconry and deanery events were also organized, and these were very well attended, despite opposition from some senior clergy. The message was an invitation to all the churches in the diocese to pause and reflect on a fundamental question: 'What is the purpose of the church?' As David Hope said at the time:

> I would like to hear about your plans for the mission entrusted to you by Christ for your locality. We have no blueprint for mission to impose. What is it that you are seeking to be and do in Christ's name?

In his key address – both on tape and when speaking at gatherings in deaneries and parishes – Archbishop David asked every parish to review how they were doing for each part of the Mission statement, and respond to him with a report showing the resulting priorities and plans. The guidelines were very simple: 'Send in two sides of A4 outlining your parish plans for future Mission action over the next four years.' He also asked parishes to consider what they should stop doing, in order to make time for new things.

His hopes and expectations were that the MAP initiative would encourage a deeper sense of unity in mission, give greater support to the local church in its discipleship, and provide deeper knowledge of how diocesan leadership could help the Church fulfil its witness and mission. During the first phase of 'Living the Gospel', a booklet was circulated to parishes to assist with their review. It commended the involvement of as many church members as possible. Some challenging questions were produced; for example, in response to the first part of the Mission statement: 'We commit ourselves to . . . Attending to God in worship, prayer, and the study of the Scriptures', Table 7.1 shows some of the questions posed in connection with this. Similar questions were asked for the other parts of the Mission statement.

Table 7.1 Some questions posed in the booklet *Living the Gospel*

Theme	Some questions to ask . . .
Service times	How complicated is your monthly timetable?
First impressions	Is there any sign that the church is open?
Inclusive/Exclusive	Access for disabled people/pram travellers?
Welcome	Who is responsible?
Preparation for worship	Are you ready to start?
Language of worship	How accessible is it?
Music	How much? Too ancient or modern?
Ambience	Is the atmosphere helpful to worship?
After the service	Can you drink coffee?

The MAPs from parishes identified where good practice could be found and this led to some parishes visiting one another, to learn from an experience, or to participate in new forms of worship. In 2001 and 2002, York archdeaconry provided three training days, principally for lay people, to focus on 'Leading All-Age Worship'. A total of 130 people attended the meetings. Large quantities of relevant resource material were made available. Those who came revealed their willingness to assist in leading worship, but expressed a real desire and need for continued support and encouragement.

Three key people were involved in forwarding the MAP initiative: John Young, the Diocesan Evangelist until his retirement in 2002, and then Paul Wordsworth (Archbishop's Mission Officer from 2001 to 2007), with support from Colin Briant, appointed as the MAP research assistant (2002–2007). It was their task to analyse maps and think through how to respond. After two years, they organized road shows for people to:

1 Show what was going on.
2 Share the many good things which were happening.
3 Highlight the 'Living the Gospel' (MAP) process (see Figure 7.1).

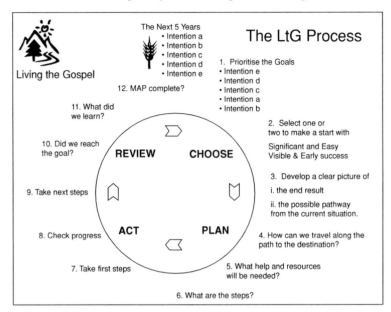

Figure 7.1 The 'Living the Gospel' process cycle

4 Rejuvenate the programme – inviting churches to go through the MAP process again, and send their MAP2s to the Archbishop.

The undoubted success of MAPs in the diocese lay in the personal invitation from the Archbishop, which led to the encouragingly large response from 80 per cent of parishes. When David Hope retired, there was some speculation about whether the MAP programme would continue. Nevertheless, during the vacancy, the senior staff asked Paul Wordsworth to start a further round of MAP. They felt that it would be timely for parishes to take part together in a review and to develop their plans for the next four-year period. An incoming archbishop would receive up-to-date information and an accurate picture of the diocese at parish and deanery levels. The leadership of the diocese would be able to make informed judgements about strategy and resources for the future.

In January 2006, at the first meeting of the Archbishop's Council under his leadership, Dr John Sentamu announced that the 'Living the Gospel' programme would continue, and the MAP process would continue as planned. It is interesting to note that Sentamu had been an Area Bishop of Stepney in the London diocese from 1996 to 2002, where he had seen at first hand how powerfully MAP had benefitted churches that had taken to heart the call to mission work. A MAP resource pack[5] was made available for parishes who requested it, which described how to produce a MAP in four sections, each with around two hours of material for groups large or small. Sessions were designed to take place over four evenings, during one full day, or as part of a parish weekend. A MAP pro-forma was designed to simplify completion and assist the analysis of returns. There were five main questions:

1 What has your experience been of working with the priorities you identified in your first MAP?
2 Do you wish to highlight any aspect that has developed particularly well, or that has been difficult to implement?
3 Have your priorities changed since your first MAP?
   (a) What do you consider to be your current strengths?
   (b) What do you consider to be your current weaknesses?
   (c) What are your current opportunities?
4 In the light of your current strengths, weaknesses and opportunities, what are your current priorities?
5 What help, advice or resources would be useful in your continued mission?

By November 2006, 222 churches had sent in their MAPs, and these were read and assessed.

Findings

- A significant number of churches attained their 2001 MAP targets and in some cases exceeded them. Only twelve churches reported that they had failed to implement the majority of the aims and objectives from MAP1 (5.4 per cent of the returns). Eight cited long vacancies of more than a year as the cause; four described pastoral reorganization which now placed them in a new setting and benefice.

- The presence of some clear guidance, a simple but focused pro-forma, and the fact that this was the second time around for many of those taking part, led to:
  - a significant number of MAPs having a deeper quality than in the first round;
  - in general, MAPs being more realistic in their priorities and opportunities;
  - fewer MAPs which were simply based on wishful thinking;
  - evidence of clarity about what was sustainable and attainable;
  - the majority of MAPs being focused on doing a few things well;
  - evidence that the MAP discussions and writing involved more people than in the first round, suggesting a deeper sense of ownership at the next review.
- Newly appointed clergy and PCCs used MAPs as a useful starting point.
- Many churches took the opportunity to report growth in key areas as part of the review.
- Examples of effective practices over a wide range of issues were provided.

Paul Wordsworth concluded that by becoming more focused, churches identified particular issues which needed attention, and these were potential opportunities for diocesan support. Paul's full report is available on the York diocesan website.

Summary of main characteristics
- Archbishop's initiative.
- Refocusing the diocese on mission.
- Top-down themes, based on new diocesan Mission statement.
- Five-year plan for the church.

- MAP process published in booklet *Living the Gospel*.
- Renewed launches after two years and five years.
- Feedback letter from Archbishop, but with a light touch.
- Two people in MAP team to help Archbishop.
- Support available on request.
- 80 per cent response from churches.
- Growth apparent as a result.

Evidence for growth

Paul Wordsworth's report draws the following conclusions:

- Mission Action Plans, consistently used, are an effective tool for enabling the local church to become more authentically 'mission shaped', and to grow according to God's plan and purpose.
    - In all churches where the MAP principles are firmly established [Category 1 churches as described earlier – around 25 per cent of the churches in York diocese], they report overall growth, often in difficult key areas such as children and young people, or increased male membership.
- MAPs have helped hundreds of churches to look more closely at how they are serving God, and what it means to be the Body of Christ in their local situation.
- Many clergy and lay people have worked collaboratively on seeking, sharing and building a united vision and purpose under God's guidance.
- Choosing, planning, acting, and reviewing, draws on the power of the Holy Spirit, encouraging wider use of the gifts of discernment, wisdom, insight, understanding, faith, and knowledge.

Lichfield 2002

A diocesan MAP – Going for Growth

In Lichfield diocese an acute financial crisis in 2002 led to the adoption of a five-year financial strategy to bring expenditure back into line with projected income. This involved the cutting of the equivalent of 50 clergy posts (out of a then total of 374 stipendiary posts). However, Bishop's Council quickly realized that cutting 50 clergy was not a long-term solution to their financial difficulties, since 50 fewer clergy would almost inevitably lead to a loss of income from the parishes, which would then trigger a further crisis and further cuts in a few years' time. Rather than simply managing decline in this way, Bishop's Council therefore made a bold decision to commission a strategy for growth, aimed at reversing the long-term numerical decline and ageing membership profile of the diocese, which was at the root of its financial problems. A significant influence on the thinking of the Bishop's Staff at this time was the publication of Bob Jackson's book *Hope for the Church* (see above).

Developing the strategy took two years of consultation with the Bishop's Staff, diocesan synod, diocesan staff, deaneries and parishes. The resulting document, *Going for Growth*, approved in October 2004, was essentially a Mission Action Plan for the diocese.

From the start *Going for Growth* was about more than simply numbers attending worship. Discipleship and community transformation were at the heart of the strategy. The three aims, adopted in 2005, were:

- to help more adults become disciples of Jesus Christ;
- to disciple more children and young people within fresh expressions of church;
- to enable churches to have greater impact in transforming their local communities.

Going for Growth built on the earlier diocesan Vision statement *Growing the Kingdom* adopted in 1995. *Growing the Kingdom* helped churches focus their work around the Kingdom of God, which is the central theme of Jesus' teaching. However, the diocese's ability to grow the Kingdom had been limited by shrinking membership and failure to attract and engage the young. *Going for Growth* aimed to focus effort on evangelism in order to win more disciples for Christ, who could share in God's mission and help grow the Kingdom and transform local communities. As the strategy came together, it developed four main strands.

The first was prayer for growth. Bishop Jonathan called the whole diocese to a day of prayer and fasting on Ash Wednesday 2005. Prayer posters were sent to every parish, and prayer cards were distributed to every church member in the diocese, with the three aims of the strategy and a prayer for growth written by Mike Bourke, Area Bishop of Wolverhampton:

> God our creator and Redeemer,
> help your church to grow in holiness, unity,
>   effectiveness and numbers.
> Draw us closer to you and to those around us.
> Give us enthusiasm in our faith,
> and wisdom in sharing it with young and old.
> Open our eyes to new opportunities,
> our lips to sing and speak of you,
> and our hearts to welcome the stranger.
> Grow your kingdom in us and in the world,
> through the intercession of our Lord Jesus Christ
> and in the power of the Holy Spirit.
> Amen.

In 2006 the focus for the day of prayer and fasting on Ash Wednesday was for more children and young people to become part of the worshipping life of the diocese.

Besides prayer, the second strand of the growth strategy was a strategic framework document for Bishop's Staff, Bishop's Council and all central diocesan staff – essentially a MAP for the diocese. Initially, some within the diocese were sceptical about a strategy for growth, and unwilling to engage with the process, but gradually over three years every sector ministry division, diocesan committee and senior staff member signed up to help deliver the strategy in some way, and it became possible to draft goals that were 'smarter' and less aspirational.

The second edition of the strategy, *A Strategic Framework for the Diocese* (approved by diocesan synod in 2005), set out five priorities within the strategy:

- Praying for growth
- Encouraging churches to grow
- Equipping people to be agents for growth
- Nurturing more children and young people in the Christian faith
- Creating a secure financial environment for lasting growth.

Under these priorities were a total of 39 specific goals, each the responsibility of a named division, council, committee or senior staff member. Progress on these goals was reviewed in 2006 and a third edition, *Going for Growth 3*, was approved in October 2006. This version included suggested actions for parishes and individuals as well as diocesan staff, and was distributed to every church member in the diocese.

The third strand of the growth strategy was to make resources available to local churches and deaneries to help them grow. One of the most effective parts of this strand was the 'Larger Churches Process', which grew out of a Travelling School in Evangelism run by Springboard across the diocese in 2001 as part of a 'Year of Evangelism and Outreach'. Having realized that most of the numerical decline in the diocese was happening in the larger churches (those with attendance over 100 adults), the area bishops invited clergy from larger churches to consultations to hear their issues, and then invited Robert Warren and Bob Jackson to lead a series of larger conferences addressing these issues. This led to a dramatic change in attendance trends in the larger churches, and a similar approach is now being implemented for churches in the 'midi' category. Another key resource that has helped stimulate growth has been the creation of the 'parish mission fund', using money from the Church Commissioners and diocesan sources to give individual grants of up to £30,000 to fund new initiatives for growth. With match-funding from other sources this has led to the creation of over 50 new posts in the diocese, mostly connected with youth and children's work. The diocesan divisions of mission, ministry and education also produced a resources guide called *Resources for Parishes and Deaneries*. This guide outlined all the ways the divisions could help parishes and deaneries plan for growth, and included a process (designed by officers from the Mission and Ministry Divisions of the diocese) for producing a Mission Action Plan – this is reproduced in Appendix 2: Version 2 – The Lichfield Process.

The fourth key strand of the strategy was to get every local church to reflect on its own mission. In the Wolverhampton Episcopal Area,[6] this was initially through day-long 'listening' visits to each cluster of parishes by the Area Bishop and the Archdeacon, which were followed up by a later return visit in which the Bishop and Archdeacon gave their reflections on what they had seen, and made suggestions to the churches to help them develop a mission plan, or MAP as it was later called. The Shrewsbury Episcopal Area was the first of the three areas of the diocese to ask every parish to produce a MAP, and has developed quite a thorough and rigorous process, which is described below. Adoption of MAPs in the Stafford Episcopal Area has been more gradual and patchy, encouraged rather than imposed from the centre.

Parish MAPs – Shrewsbury Area

In 2004, Alan Smith, Area Bishop of Shrewsbury in Lichfield diocese, wrote to all his parishes asking them to draw up a MAP, in order to 'encourage all churches to have mission and evangelism on their agendas in practice as well as in theory'. He said that the MAP would be at the centre of discussions during a pastoral visit, and also used as a basis for discussion about a new priest during a vacancy. Parishes were asked first to review every part of parish life and see how each part could be part of mission and evangelism, and second to put in place a small number of practical and achievable initiatives that would lead to growth. The Bishop, Archdeacon of Salop, and Rural Deans pledged to give time and energy to work with the clergy, PCCs and congregations on the task.

A MAP pro-forma was defined as follows:

1 A description of the parish – the area that God has entrusted you to care for, reflecting on its population, schools, places of work, sheltered housing, etc.
2 A description of the church, including its people and its resources (such as buildings).
3 A review of all that is already going on in the life of the church and how each part of it may be able to evolve and develop in order to grow.
4 A Vision statement: 'Where do you believe God is leading you and what does he want you to do?'
5 The plan – a small number of events, courses or initiatives for growth. In particular, churches were asked to consider:
   (a) GROWING TOGETHER – through Worship and Prayer
   (b) GROWING UP – through Teaching and Nurture
   (c) GROWING MORE – through Outreach and Evangelism
   (d) GROWING OUT – through Justice and Care
6 Actions which need to be SMART.
7 A part of the Mission Action Plan was to reflect on the ministry resources that were needed and how these could be developed in each parish.
8 The Plan should also need to reflect on how the appropriate financial resources could be raised to ensure the future growth and effectiveness of the parish.

Parishes were encouraged to appoint a consultant (either lay or ordained) to be a critical friend – the sort of person who would ask intelligent and thoughtful questions about the Mission Action Plan in a supportive way.

Further, the intended follow-up was published: each year, the PCC would have a visit from the Bishop, the Archdeacon, the Rural Dean or one of the sector ministers in order to review progress, to learn from their experiences and to work with them to redefine the aims in the light of the experience of the previous year. One year on, the review work was further supported by written feedback to parishes and senior clergy by external experts/consultants. These reports were positive and encouraging, and preceded a telephone call with the vicar.

Summary of main characteristics

- Area Bishop's initiative.
- Refocusing the area on mission and growth.
- Top-down definition of growth: Together, Up, More Out.
- Churches asked to work out a five-year vision, and plans for one year and five years.
- MAP process published in letters to clergy and PCCs.
- Feedback: written report from consultant and discussion with senior clergy.
- Support available on request.

Evidence for growth

Looking at the statistics for Lichfield diocese over the period 2003–2008, the figures do not (yet) show an increase in usual adult Sunday attendance. However, there are a number of significant encouragements:

- The long-term downward trend has now levelled out – over the period 2000–2008 the annual rate of loss of usual Sunday attendance has dropped from 3.0 per cent to just 0.3 per cent (see Figure 7.2).
- Weekday attendance (as measured by the October count) has grown significantly – by 27 per cent in the four years 2004–2008. Although the weekday numbers are smaller, the big growth in midweek attendance more than compensates for the slight loss in Sunday attendance.
- The change in trend for the usual Sunday attendance of children is much clearer – having been falling faster than the rate

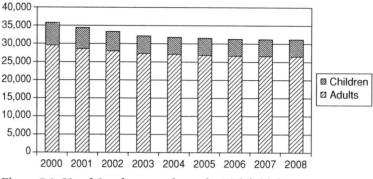

Figure 7.2 Usual Sunday attendance for Lichfield diocese

of decline for adults for many years, over the last two years the number of children has actually grown slightly. This means that churches are now growing younger, rather than shrinking older as in previous years.

The remarkable thing is that this significant improvement in the attendance trends of both adults and children has been achieved at the same time as cutting 47 stipendiary posts in the diocese, which would normally have led to an accelerating rate of decline.[7] This is clear testimony that the diocesan MAP, *Going for Growth*, has achieved measurable results in two of its three stated aims.

What is harder to identify from the figures for Lichfield diocese is a contrast between attendance in those parishes which have produced a good MAP and those that haven't. MAP has been introduced differently in each of the three areas of the diocese. Shrewsbury Area was the first to introduce MAP, with a top-down requirement on every parish to produce a MAP, followed up with an annual 'inspection' visit by a different member of diocesan staff. This has led to a high level of compliance, at least on paper, but may not have won hearts and minds.

By contrast, in Wolverhampton Area the initial approach was for the Bishops and Archdeacons to spend whole days in

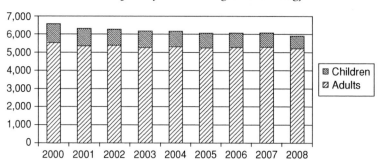

Figure 7.3 Usual Sunday attendance, Shrewsbury Area of Lichfield diocese

every cluster 'coming alongside' the clergy in their mission, and only recently have parishes been asked to produce a formal MAP. The introduction of MAP has been more bottom-up, following a process of listening. Bob Jackson[8] concludes that combining MAP with a cycle of day-long visits from the senior staff and finding external consultants to advise and work alongside parishes is the most effective combination to help local churches to grow. The attendance trends in Shrewsbury Area and Walsall Archdeaconry are shown in graphs produced by Bob Jackson in his review of *Going for Growth*, and are reproduced with permission (see Figures 7.3 and 7.4).[9]

The contrasting results of Shrewsbury and Walsall Areas over the last five years are doubtless influenced by many different factors. However, they may suggest Bishop David Hope was right in his initial approach in London diocese – listening to the needs of local churches, and making MAP something that was encouraged, not imposed. As he commented in his interview with us, 'We didn't force it – I thought if it was good it would spread by word of mouth.'

The evidence from Lichfield diocese is that a clear diocesan MAP has made a significant difference to the performance of the diocese, and that at parish level MAP can be a very fruitful tool – especially where churches engage because they are

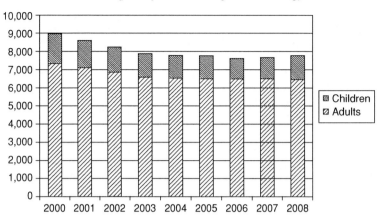

Figure 7.4 Usual Sunday attendance, Walsall Area of Lichfield diocese

inspired rather than required to do so, and where members of the senior staff and other trained consultants come alongside the local leadership to listen and to provide consistent advice and support over a period of years.

Blackburn 2004

Nicholas Reade was installed as Bishop of Blackburn in March 2004, and right from the start, he was keen to introduce MAP. He had discussed his priorities with his Archbishop – Prayer, Holiness and Mission – and David Hope had told him about MAP. Blackburn diocese had been declining in numbers by an average of 2.5 per cent per year for the past 20 years, and he was keen to reverse this trend during his time in the diocese. During the first six months, he had mentioned MAP in the diocesan magazine and in sermons during visits to parishes, but the initial response was disappointing – he soon realized that a change of culture was needed. Under his chairmanship he set up a special MAP group which he felt had the necessary experience and skills: two members of Bishop's Staff, five incumbents, the diocesan secretary, the directors of ministry and mission,

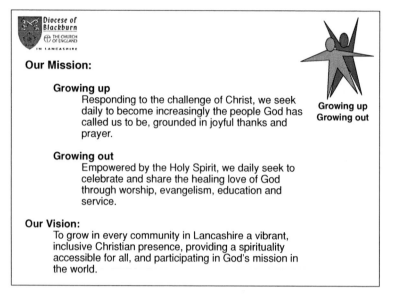

Our Mission:

Growing up
Responding to the challenge of Christ, we seek daily to become increasingly the people God has called us to be, grounded in joyful thanks and prayer.

Growing out
Empowered by the Holy Spirit, we daily seek to celebrate and share the healing love of God through worship, evangelism, education and service.

Our Vision:
To grow in every community in Lancashire a vibrant, inclusive Christian presence, providing a spirituality accessible for all, and participating in God's mission in the world.

Figure 7.5 Blackburn diocese Mission and Vision statements, 2004

and a facilitator. These last three became the working group and engine of the team – suggesting ways forward and driving the actions.

The group put forward a new Mission statement and Vision statement for the diocese (see Figure 7.5), and this was accepted by the Bishop's Council. A logo was designed to help with communication, and publicity and training materials were prepared. These included a bookmark, a lapel badge and posters for parishes.

In addition, booklets about MAP were produced: an introduction to MAP – 'Putting Mission on the MAP', and a description of the annual MAP process. This was very similar to the York cycle except that 'Vision' was added as the key part of the Choose phase. The principle here is that a five-year vision reinforces the desire to discover God's will for the church, it provides a good basis for working out priorities and it eases the way for change, drawing people to work together (see Figure 7.6).

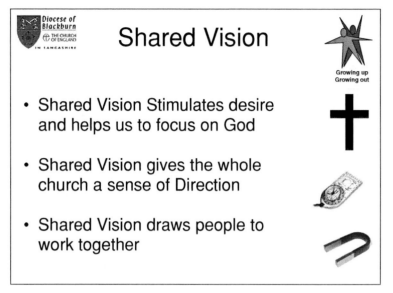

Figure 7.6 The impact of 'Shared Vision'

All these materials were distributed during a MAP launch at the cathedral in March 2005, along with the 'Bishop's MAP' – which had been produced by the MAP group and endorsed by the Bishop's Staff and the diocesan synod. This communicated the priorities and actions of the Bishop, his Staff and the diocesan departments. Resources could also be downloaded from the diocesan website, and church facilitators were trained and made available on request. The Bishop preached about mission and MAP, and requested that copies of parish MAPs be sent to him within a year, so that he could keep in touch with parish plans, and so that he could pray for their work. He sent an acknowledgement back to the parish when a MAP was received, followed later by a short letter giving his observations. He and other members of Bishop's Staff frequently mentioned MAP during visits to parishes. After 12 months, 85 per cent of parishes had sent their MAPs to the Bishop. A second Bishop's MAP was published in March 2006, together with an Ad

Clerum[10] inviting churches to repeat the MAP process cycle and send their second MAPs to the Bishop.

A further significant step was taken in 2006. The MAP group were keen to bring clergy together to learn about the Bishop's vision for growth, and to train them in using the MAP process. When considering how they would put together a suitable course, the national four-day course 'Leading Your Church into Growth' came to their attention. The working group – which had now become four people – arranged to attend a course to assess it. They found that the course was entirely compatible with the MAP process, and started a discussion with the course leaders about how they could get large numbers of diocesan clergy to attend the course over a two-year period. As a result, an agreement was reached whereby the diocese was given a licence to run the course, using their own trainers, and one of these was appointed also to the national core team. The first course was run in September 2006 and the evaluation by participants was excellent. Further courses were planed for the following two years.

In 2007, Bishop Nicholas decided that the time had come to celebrate the progress so far with the members of the MAP group, but also to inform them of his plan to dissolve the group, and to use the regular diocesan bodies and groups to lead MAP work. Growth strategy soon became a fixed item on the Bishop's Staff agenda, and church MAPs were seen as a central part of it. The title 'Going for Growth' was chosen for the diocesan initiative, and the first strategic plan was published in March 2007, using the annual MAP process. This replaced the 'Bishop's MAP'. In his introduction to the document, Bishop Nicholas said:

> I have been working with Bishop's Staff to produce a coherent plan for the development of the ministry and mission of our diocese over the next five years. In planning for the future, we have consulted widely with clergy and laity and drawn together

a growth strategy for the next five years. This consists of consolidating existing good work while also initiating new areas of
sustainable growth. A great deal of work has gone into this and
I hope you will read and reflect on the strategy. However, this is
an evolving process, and we will review the actions frequently,
and the overall strategy annually. We welcome observations and
comments from all groups and individuals.

I regularly give thanks for the excellent work being carried
out in a large number of our parishes, not least with the ongoing Mission Action Plan initiative. As we continue to develop
specific areas of mission, I feel that we are now in a position to
develop further our plans and look with greater confidence to
the future. I therefore encourage you to continue to make every
effort to proclaim the gospel as best as you can, and to share the
love of God not only amongst the people of our congregations
but also and especially with those in society who are searching
for new purpose and life.

This comes with much prayer for you and my thanks for all
that you do.

He again asked parishes to go through the annual MAP cycle
and to send him their MAPs. The booklet went on to describe
the strategy topics that the Bishop's Staff developed – under
four headings: Prayer, Parishes, People and Leaders, and Diocesan
resources – as part of an overall growth strategy. The booklet
shared some examples of good news that had happened over the
last year. Moreover, the booklet also announced that in order
to further support and encourage mission work in parishes,
the Bishops and Archdeacons planned to visit all parishes in the
following two to three years with an offer to lead an appropriate mission activity, while also making time to be with and
listen to people. These visits are to become known as 'Growing
up Growing out Days'.

At the end of the second year, 70 per cent of parishes had
sent their Maps to the Bishop. Some parishes found that the
annual cycle was too frequent, either because their programmes

were longer term or because of workload. Nevertheless, the annual cycle was still recommended, even if the 'Choose' phase was done with a light touch. It was pointed out that the MAP process has a kind of rolling five-year horizon, where five-year priorities can be updated, and one-year priorities are always fresh. Also, because for many people strategy planning was a new activity, it was important to experience and learn about the process year on year.

The 'Going for Growth' and MAP activities continued for another year, and the 'Going for Growth 2' plan was published in March 2008. By then, many of the growth topics of the previous year had been either completed or taken in to the normal running of the diocese, so a new approach was taken by the Bishop's Staff. They had analysed all the MAPs that had been received the previous year, and found that the top three items adopted as church priorities were concerned with Prayer, Nurture Courses and Children. They considered how they and the diocesan resources could support churches in these areas, and, as a result, three project teams were set up, each under the leadership of a bishop. The goals and plans were published in 'Going for Growth 2'. This also had encouraging news for everyone: the rate of decline in attendance over the previous year had slowed down significantly, and there was evidence that churches that had been working hard on mission activities were showing numerical growth.

The Bishop's Staff began their next review cycle in November 2008, and this time they were looking for a tool that would introduce more rigour than the usual SWOT analysis. Their facilitator came up with an adaptation of the European Excellence model, and a team from the Bishop's Staff developed this further. Using this tool, they discovered among other things that there was a problem with the Vision statement: it was not well known and was not being used to inspire growth priorities across the diocese. So the Staff developed a new Vision statement:

Growing in faith and prayer
transforming communities
in the power of the Holy Spirit.

By March 2009, a slimmer more attractive 'Going for Growth 3' booklet was distributed to all church members, which contained a letter from Bishop Nicholas, an explanation of the new Vision statement and news about the three growth priorities. Progress on these had been encouraging, and the Bishop's Staff announced that work would continue for a further year. The booklet also contained encouraging news about attendance trends – see the next section.

Summary of main characteristics

- Bishop's initiative.
- Focusing the diocese on mission.
- Special group set up to introduce MAP.
- MAP process published in booklet, and other publicity materials were used.
- Bishop's MAP produced for the first two years, followed by three 'Going for Growth' strategy booklets.
- Annual plan recommended for each church.
- Feedback letter from the Bishop, but with a light touch.
- Two people assigned to assist the Bishop with responses.
- Support available on request.
- 85 per cent response from churches in the first year (2005–06).
- Growth apparent as a result.

Evidence for growth

After one year of the MAP initiative, the Bishop's Staff and MAP group had lots of anecdotal evidence that MAP was making a difference in those churches who were engaged in the process. After two years, the 2006 'usual Sunday attendance' (uSa) figures were available for further analysis. A comparison

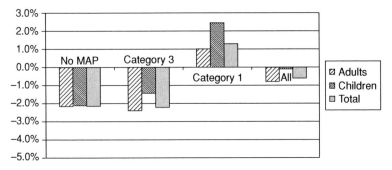

Figure 7.7 Comparing uSa growth rates 2005–06 for churches in Blackburn diocese

of attendance trends for churches that submitted MAPs in 2005 with those who did not showed no significant difference between the two groups. However, when a more detailed analysis was done to compare Category 1 churches with Category 3 churches (see p. 100), and both these were compared with those who did not submit MAPs (which would be Category 2 or Category 4), the chart shown in Figure 7.7 was produced.

The chart shows an encouraging result, especially for children. This was communicated as good news in the diocese, but celebrations were a little muted. Was this a flash in the pan? Would news about attendance numbers distract from the main message that growth is about 'Growing up and Growing out'? Despite the result being statistically significant, the Bishop's Staff were cautious.

After a further year, the 2007 attendance figures were available, and the above analysis was repeated, using the original categories (see Figure 7.8). The positive results of Category 1 churches are enhanced, whereas the decline in the other churches is more negative; again, a significant result.

More analysis was done and two further comparisons were made. One intriguing question was, 'Does attending the "Leading Your Church into Growth" (LYCiG) course make a difference to growth?' The chart (see Figure 7.9) compares 2007

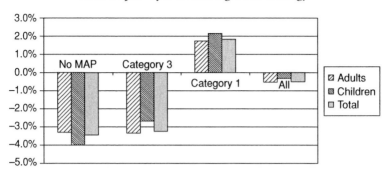

Figure 7.8 Comparing uSa growth rates 2006–07 for churches in Blackburn diocese

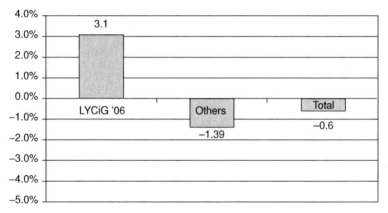

Figure 7.9 Growth rates for churches in Blackburn diocese 2006–07: impact on uSa of LYCiG

data for churches whose clergy attended the first LYCiG course in 2006 with others, and indicates that growth in attendance *can* be influenced by training about growth and the quality of mission planning.

The second comparison arose in connection with the 'Child Friendly Church Award' (CFCA). From 2005 onwards, churches were encouraged to become more child friendly, and the CFCA award scheme was introduced. The process of making improvements and gaining the award can take up to two years. So,

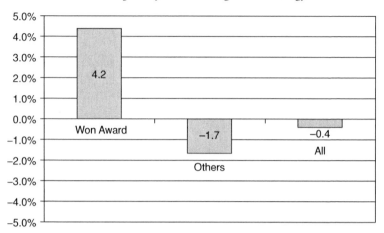

Figure 7.10 Growth rates for churches in Blackburn diocese 2006–07: impact on uSa of the 'Child Friendly Church Award'

another question was: 'Is there evidence that the change in children's attendance was more positive for those churches who were in the CFCA process?' Figure 7.10 shows the percentage change in uSa in 2006–07 for those churches in Blackburn diocese who won the award, compared with others – and indicates that growth in children's attendance *can* be influenced by training about how to work with children in church. There was no significant difference for adult attendance.

The overall conclusion for the Blackburn diocese is that the Growth/MAP initiative has made a significant difference to the attendance trend for usual Sunday attendance, especially for those churches that have responded positively to the Bishop's call for Mission Action Plans.

8

MAP resources and further information

The Church MAP website

The Church MAP website <http://www.churchmaps.co.uk> provides a very valuable resource for those engaged in Mission Action Planning at church, area or diocesan levels. The site aims to be a resource for those who are already engaged with MAP or are thinking about starting MAP work. The idea for the site came from a meeting between Mike Chew and Peter Hill, who at that time was undertaking research into MAP as part of his Ph.D. studies. Roger Longworth, a long-time friend of Mike and former churchwarden of St John's Church at Baxenden, set up the site and is the current webmaster.

It is worth noting that the logo for the site (see Figure 8.1) signifies that MAP can lead to the growth of Christians and derives from a synthesis of the desire for mission work together with a process for action planning.

All the content of the site has been supplied by church organizations or churches that are willing to share and learn together, and it is expanding all the time. The site currently has information provided by the dioceses of Blackburn, Carlisle, Chichester, Ely, Exeter, Guildford, Leicester, Lichfield, Llandaff, London, Newcastle, Norwich, Portsmouth, Ripon and Leeds, Southwell, St Asaph, Wakefield and York. Their information can be accessed either through their diocesan pages or via another menu which groups the documents in the areas of 'Starting up',

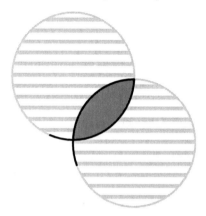

**Figure 8.1 The Church MAP website logo (<http://www.
churchmaps. co.uk>)**

'MAP process', 'Training Resources', 'Follow up', 'Growth Strategy'
and 'MAP examples'. The menu for all these documents has one
or two sentences summarizing their content. The site also has
handy links to the mission pages of diocesan websites, a News
section and an email link to the site managers.

Recommended books

(Note: CHP = Church House Publishing)

Paul Bayes, Tim Sledge, John Holbrook, Mark Rylands, Martin
Seeley, *Mission Shaped Parish* (London: CHP, 2006).
Stephen Cottrell, *Hit the Ground Kneeling* (London: CHP,
2008).
Graham Cray et al., *Mission Shaped Church Report* (London:
CHP, 2004).
Mark Ireland and Mike Booker, *Evangelism – which way now?*
(London: CHP, 2006).
Bob Jackson, *The Road to Growth* (London: CHP, 2005).
John Kotter, *Leading Change* (Harvard Business School Press,
1996).

Eugene Peterson, *The Gift: Reflections on Christian Ministry* (London: Marshall Pickering, 1993).

Yvonne Richmond, Nick Spencer, Rob Frost, Anne Richards, Mark Ireland, Steven Croft, *Evangelism in a Spiritual Age* (London: CHP, 2005).

Peter Senge, *The Fifth Discipline* (New York: Doubleday, 1994).

Alan Smith, *God Shaped Mission: Theological and Practical Perspectives from the Rural Church* (Norwich: Canterbury Press, 2008).

Robert Warren, *The Healthy Churches Handbook* (London: CHP, 2004).

Garry Wills, *Certain Trumpets: The Nature of Leadership* (New York: Touchstone, 1995).

A quick read

Grove Booklets can be purchased for £2.95 each, or downloaded from <http://www.grovebooks.co.uk> – so they won't break the bank!

Paul Bayes, *Mission Shaped Church* (EV 67).

Jim Currin, *How to Develop a Mission Strategy* (EV 68).

Alison Gilchrist, *Creating a Culture of Welcome in the Local Church* (EV 66).

Alan Howe, *Leading Ordinary Churches into Growth* (EV 70).

Geoff Pearson, *Towards the Conversion of England* (EV 71).

Richard Williams and Mark Tanner, *Developing Visionary Leadership* (R 17).

Meetings for facilitators and mission enablers

From time to time, the authors arrange a meeting of all those interested in MAP at diocesan, deanery, district or area levels to share and learn from each others' experiences. The first such meeting was held at Mark Ireland's church in Wellington in September 2008. It was attended by 18 Anglicans and Methodists from all over the UK. If any reader would like to be notified about future meetings, please register your interest by sending an email to churchmaps@gmail.com.

Facilitator support for churches

We recommend that churches consider using the services of a facilitator during the Review and Choose phases of the MAP process. Facilitators bring a fresh pair of eyes and a critical friend to help think through the church's situation, strategy and vision. They are skilled in the various approaches to conducting a review of church health, and can guide church leaders through the Vision process. It is sometimes difficult for church ministers to ask their council members difficult and challenging questions – but a facilitator can.

Many dioceses, Methodist districts and other denominations now provide such facilitators to their churches on request at no cost, and so the first person to contact if you need a facilitator is your diocesan missioner, district evangelism enabler, or equivalent person. There are also many independent consultants/ facilitators who usually provide a service for a reasonable fee. As a last resort, the Church MAP website may be able to help you to find a facilitator in your area, or arrange for you to receive telephone consultation. In this case, email enquiries should be directed to churchmaps@gmail.com.

9

Conclusions

————◆•◆•◆————

Sanctified common sense

Trust in the LORD with all your heart and lean not on your own understanding; in all your ways acknowledge him, and he will make your paths straight.   (Proverbs 3.5–6)

In Chapter 1 we asked whether MAP is just another fad or tool taken from the world of business. Having carefully researched the subject, and having worked at applying the principles in our own parishes and dioceses, we have found that the MAP process is really a form of sanctified common sense – like the Wisdom literature of the Old Testament. It is interesting that the writer of Proverbs felt able to borrow freely from an earlier Egyptian text *Instruction of Amen-em-ope* for his 'Sayings of the Wise' in 22.17—23.11. In a similar way the principles of MAP draw on the insights of today's secular writers in the field of leadership and strategic planning. However, just as the writer of Proverbs adapts his material to fit his clear Israelite faith in the true God, so MAP takes thinking about strategic planning and puts it in the context of prayer and seeking to discern the will of God for his Church. In this way MAP becomes much more than just a management process, but rather a spiritual exercise. As a church learns to take time to listen to God and to reflect on its experience, so it is able to discern the big picture – how the day-to-day life of that parish can be part of the *missio dei,* the work which God by his Holy Spirit is doing in his world today.

Even though MAP is a common-sense approach, some churches will still find it hard work, especially if their leadership has not got previous experience of this way of working. However, now that MAP has been around for over ten years there is a solid body of experience and good practice which churches can learn from. We hope that this book, and the Church MAP website, will help hard-pressed church leaders to learn from the experience of others without having to reinvent the wheel. We have met a lot of wise people who are willing to share their hard-won experience, so we would particularly encourage those new to this process to find an external consultant or critical friend to help them. As we said at the end of the last chapter, diocesan missioners or Methodist evangelism enablers (or equivalents in other denominations) are in a good position to advise on someone suitable locally. Alternatively, we will do our best to help.

Keep at it!

Too often churches – like government departments! – come up with new ideas and move on to new initiatives without ever giving time for things they have started to bear fruit, or taking time to review and evaluate their experience. Our research has also shown that MAP is by no means a 'quick-fix'. Producing a MAP mustn't be just a one-off exercise, or it will become yet another wish-list that gathers dust in the vicar's study. The process needs to be repeated regularly, ideally every year, with quality time given to the review phase, so that we check up on what we have done, learn from our experience, and revise our MAP in the light of what we have learnt. Going through the MAP cycle regularly helps a church to get better at the process, and will mean that the goals in the MAP gradually become 'smarter' and more robust, and less of a wish-list. If a job's worth doing, it's worth doing well, and this means taking time to learn the skills involved – those churches that just go through the motions so that they have a piece of paper to send off to the bishop might as well not bother.

Just as physical health comes from a healthy lifestyle and regular exercise, rather than a crash diet or sudden over-exertion, so making MAP a regular part of parish life for the long term, not a one-off burst of activity, is the best way to foster the health of a church.

Keeping the main thing the main thing

Over 25 years helping to lead local churches we have learnt that 'the main thing is to keep the main thing the main thing'. Too often church councils and clergy allow ourselves to get diverted onto secondary agendas – whether moving pews, women bishops, sexuality or maintaining built heritage. MAP is a really useful process because it keeps bringing us back to what the church is here for – to share in God's mission in the world. A clear *Mission* statement can help to define the purpose of the church (though many Mission statements can read a bit like platitudes!) but developing a clear *Vision* statement that defines the direction the church is heading in is even more important. If this is worked on by a large cross section of the congregation and communicated across the whole fellowship, then vision becomes the vision of the church, rather than simply the vision of the minister. A clear and inspiring Vision statement has great value as a touchstone in all discussions about other issues – 'How will this help us fulfil our Vision statement?' is the key question we need to keep asking.

Can you measure the effectiveness of MAP?

In previous chapters we have seen solid evidence that churches that produce a good quality MAP find it helps them to grow numerically. However, the process of bringing a church together around a common vision is of huge value in itself, whether or not the numbers begin to rise afterwards. The primary aim of MAP is *not* to increase the numbers in church – there are other ways to do that – but to improve the health of the church. Increasing numbers are a sign of health, not an end in themselves. Businesses or banks which focus exclusively on maximizing the bottom line can easily go wrong, as the recent banking crisis has shown. A healthy bottom line should be the reward for doing the right things rather than aim of the organization; likewise in churches, increasing attendance should be a sign of health, not the chief aim of the organization. A healthy church is more attractive to outsiders and therefore more likely to grow, but a healthy church is one which does not make its own growth its primary objective.

The primary aims of the church must always be to glorify God, to grow his Kingdom, to help people of every background become disciples of Jesus, and to show the love of Jesus to those in need. If we attend to our primary calling, God will look after the rest. As St Paul wrote, 'I sowed the seed, Apollos watered it, but God made it grow.'

Appendix 1
MAP workshop outline

———•◆•———

The following is an outline programme, along the lines that many churches have followed. It should not be regarded as fixed, because flexibility is always needed to tailor it to the needs of each church. It takes place over two 3-hour sessions – two evenings or an away-day. There is a need for some work in advance – for example, a community Mission Audit. The leader may ask someone to act as a timekeeper – to let him or her know how each session is going compared with the plan. Sometimes, a church may invite a facilitator or consultant to assist with the process.

Session 1: MAP Process – Review

During the review phase, the objective is to discover your current state and to listen to God, your community and your existing members. Avoid the temptation to talk about new actions until this phase is complete and you have developed a Vision statement in the next session.

Session topic	Suggested timing
Prayer, worship and listening to God	10 minutes
What do we mean by 'Mission' (Theological reflection)	5 minutes
Introduction: The MAP process	10 minutes

Either

1 Revised SWOT Review using Post-It notes (see below)   45 minutes
    10 minutes explanation
    15 minutes individual work
    20 minutes sharing together

Appendix 1 MAP workshop outline

Session topic	Suggested timing
Or	
2 'Growing Healthy Churches' assessment	60 minutes
20 minutes explanation	
20 minutes scoring	
20 minutes feedback/discussion	
Values: explanation	5 minutes
Values: plenary discussion about which values are a priority for this church to work on	10 minutes
Listening to the community – input	10 minutes
Feedback of survey results e.g. demographics, interview notes etc.	
Listening to the church members – input	10 minutes
Feedback of survey results	
Listening to God	30 minutes
What would God say about our church today?	
(Group prayer, discussions, then sharing)	
Conclusions from this review	20 minutes
Group discussions to share what has been learnt	
Conclusions: Plenary discussion	20 minutes
Sharing the conclusions of the session	
Use flip charts, write these up afterwards and distribute to members	
Closing prayers	5 minutes

Using Post-It! notes – in groups

They can be used in a variety of brainstorming situations. Here is how it works . . .

1 Working on their own, each group member writes their response on yellow notes – one for each point.
2 When finished (or after 30 minutes maximum) each member is invited to share their responses by sticking their notes on a wall (or similar).
3 As more members share, one member, or the facilitator, groups similar notes together. A heading for these groups is proposed and agreed.
4 At the end, the group can visually conclude what are the key factors, and a consensus is arrived at.

Session 2: MAP Process – Choose

Session topic	Suggested timing
Prayer, worship and listening to God	15 minutes
Teaching on the 'Mission statement'	5 minutes
Group discussions: 'What are the key ingredients of our new/revised Mission statement?'	20 minutes
Sharing together, and appointing small group to work on the statement after today	10 minutes
Teaching on 'Vision'	10 minutes
Group discussions: 'What are the key ingredients of the new Vision statement?'	20 minutes
Sharing together, and appointing a small group of leaders to work on the statement	20 minutes
Plenary discussion about the priorities to work on in the next year (first, decide the maximum number of strategic priorities that you can cope with, and keep to it!)	30 minutes

Plenary discussion to develop goals for each
    priority area – SMART and owned   30 minutes
Conclusions: Plenary discussion   15 minutes
    Sharing the conclusions of the session
    Use flipcharts, write these up afterwards
      and distribute to members
Closing prayers   5 minutes

Depending on how much time the above takes in practice, it may also be possible to cover the next stage (Plan), but, often, this is done in a group after the first sessions. The group is led by the owner of the relevant goal, and the members are appointed by the minister, after consultation with the owner. Before the plan is finally agreed, an overall check of resources should be carried out. Is any person or facility overloaded? Is the plan as a whole achievable?

Finally, the Plan for each goal should be presented at the next church council meeting, and agreed after discussion.

Appendix 2
MAP templates

Version 1: The Blackburn MAP template

Church:	Location:	Date:

Stage 1: Review

Our strengths 'Isn't it good that . . .'	
Our weaknesses 'Isn't it a pity that . . .'	
Our opportunities 'Wouldn't it be good if . . .'	

Our Mission values What influences and motivates us . . .	
Last MAP actions **completed**	
Last MAP actions **not completed**	

Stage 2: Choose

Our Mission statement Our purpose/reason for being here	
Our Vision statement What we believe God is calling our church to become in five years' time	
Our Priority goals for this year A maximum of 3 for this next year	1. 2. 3.

Stage 3: Plan

Actions			Who	When
1	a			
	b			
	c			

Date published: _____ When will your MAP be reviewed? _____

Version 2: The Lichfield process

Preparing the Way
⇒ Decide who will be involved in the process (try to allocate time in existing PCC meetings, so that you are not consuming even more energy on planning).
⇒ Carefully study the introductory paper.
⇒ Decide if some outside help would be beneficial in the process (a consultant?).

Where are we now?
⇒ You may find it helpful to view the video '**Restoring Hope in our Church**'
⇒ Gain a clear understanding of the communities in which the Parish is set (Parish Audit?)
⇒ Take a critical and honest look at the Church Community (Perhaps using the Springboard Resource *Principles of growing a healthy Church*).

Discerning Church vocation – what is the Mission that God is calling us to?
(Growing Together, Growing Up, Growing More, Growing Out – see section A.1)
⇒ Prayer and Bible Study John 15.1–8, Luke 8.1–8
⇒ What is God saying to us:
  • What is God calling us to be in this Parish?
  • What is God calling us to do in this Parish?
  • Who is God calling us to do this with?
⇒ How will this vocation produce growth in our Church?
⇒ Is there scope for planting a new congregation? Mid week? Not in the church building?

What Ministries are we already involved in?
⇒ Are these Ministries about 'Maintenance' or 'Mission'?
⇒ What can we stop doing to release energy for Kingdom Growth Initiatives?

What Ministries do we need to fulfil this Mission?
⇒ Do we have these Ministries?
⇒ Do we have the gifts to develop these Ministries?
⇒ What help do we need to develop these Ministries?

Write the Mission Action Plan
⇒ What will we commit ourselves to do or be:
  – Over the next five years?
  – During the next 12 months?
⇒ How will we measure our progress?
⇒ The demands of the MAP must not be beyond what we have the energy or capacity to do or to develop.
⇒ It might be that the MAP shows our calling to do what we are already doing, but with fresh vision and energy.
⇒ SMART is an overriding principle:
  Plans must be Specific and documented
  Outcomes must be Measurable, revise objectives if necessary
  Proposals must be Achievable
  Actions must be Resourced
  To enable proper review Time boundaries are essential.

Notes

Preface

[1] Some 25 per cent of the Internet traffic on our website <http://www.churchmaps.co.uk> is from overseas.

1. Setting the scene

[1] In other words 'no change': 'The maxim of the British people is "Business as usual"' – Sir Winston Churchill.
[2] From the training material of Exeter diocese <http://www.churchmaps.co.uk>.
[3] J. Adair, *Not Bosses, but Leaders* (Guildford: Talbot Adair Press, 1987).
[4] Interview with the authors, 6 June 2008.
[5] James Kouzes and Barry Posner, *The Leadership Challenge* (San Francisco: Josey-Bass Publishers, 1995).

2. Reflecting on our experience – at St John's, Baxenden

[1] Matthew 28.18–20.
[2] John Kotter, *Leading Change* (Harvard Business School Press, 1996).

3. Theological Reflections on MAP

[1] Jeremiah 29.11; Psalm 138.8.
[2] Luke 9.1–6; 10.1–17.
[3] Luke 14.28, 31 (NRSV).
[4] Acts 16.6–10.
[5] The New International Dictionary of New Testament Theology (Carlisle: Paternoster Press, 1976), vol. 2, p. 129.

[6] Christian Schwarz, *Natural Church Development Handbook* (St Charles, IL: Churchsmart Resources, 1996).

[7] Acts 6.7.

[8] Avery Dulles, *Models of the Church* (2nd edn; Dublin: Gill and McMillan, 1989).

[9] David Bosch, *Transforming Mission* (Maryknoll: Orbis, 1991), p. 1.

[10] P. Schutz, *Zwischen Nil und Kaukasus* (Munich: Kaiser Verlag, 1930), p. 245, cited in (and translated by) Bosch, *Transforming Mission*, p. 10.

[11] Bosch, *Transforming Mission*, pp. 512–18.

[12] Bosch, *Transforming Mission*, pp. 10–11.

[13] Cited in Bosch, *Transforming Mission*, p. 9.

[14] It is also found in the Meissen, Porvoo and Reuilly statements with the continental Protestant churches. See also Dulles, *Models of the Church*, pp. 58–70.

[15] Bosch, *Transforming Mission*, p. 11.

[16] *Mission-shaped Church* (London: Church House Publishing, 2004), pp. 82–3; copyright © The Archbishops' Council.

[17] George Lings, one of the authors of the report, has made a similar point.

[18] Athanasius, *Life of St Antony* (reprinted by St Antony Monastery, 1992).

[19] J. Verkuyl, *Contemporary Missiology* (Grand Rapids: Eerdmans, 1978); G. van Rheenan, *Missions* (Grand Rapids: Zondervan, 1996).

4. How does MAP fit with other recent approaches to mission?

[1] A major interdenominational initiative in Birmingham in 1992 adopted the bold vision to evangelize Britain by planting 20,000 new churches by the year 2000. The title of the conference was 'Discipling a Whole Nation' (DAWN). The DAWN strategy originated in the Phlippines in 1974, but had come to prominence in 1989 at Lausanne II, an international conference on world evangelization.

[2] Ann Morisey, *Journeying Out* (London: Continuum, 2006); *Faithful Cities*, The Commisssion on Urban Life and Family (London:

Church House Publishing, 2006); Mark Greene, *Supporting Christians at Work* (Sheffield: Administry, 2001).

5. Producing a Mission Action Plan – step by step

1 Tim Dearborn, *Beyond Duty: A Passion for Christ, a Heart for Mission* (Monrovia, CA: MARC, 1989).
2 Diocese of Llandaff, Church in Wales.
3 Usually known as 'Archdeacons' Visitations in the Church of England, when churchwardens take their vows for the coming year. However, bishops occasionally preside and speak at these, when they are known as 'Primary Visitations'.
4 Antoine de Saint-Exupéry, *The Little Prince,* trans. Richard Howard (1943; reprinted New York: Harvest, 2000).
5 Local community information is available on the National Statistics website <http://www.statistics.gov.uk>.
6 Robert Warren, *The Healthy Churches' Handbook* (London: Church House Publishing, 2004).
7 Christian Schwarz, *Natural Church Development Handbook* (St Charles, IL: Churchsmart Resources, 1996).
8 See, for example, the Healthy Churches website <http://www.healthychurch.co.uk>.
9 *Mission-shaped Church* (London: Church House Publishing, 2004).
10 Peter Senge, *The Fifth Discipline* (New York: Doubleday, 1990), p. 205.
11 Stephen Cottrell, *Hit the Ground Kneeling: Seeing Leadership Differently* (London: Church House Publishing, 2009).
12 Senge, *Fifth Discipline*, p. 205.

7. MAP as part of a diocesan growth strategy

1 See Bob Jackson, 'A Capital Idea: Church Growth in the Diocese of London – Causes and Implications', available on the London diocesan website or on <http://www.churchmaps.co.uk>.
2 *Hope for the Church* (London: Church House Publishing, 2002) and *The Road to Growth* (London: Church House Publishing, 2005).

3 Assuming growth in mission activities in a church is eventually reflected in growth in attendance.

4 Neil Evans is Director of Professional Development in London diocese.

5 The material is available on the York diocesan website at <http://www.churchmaps.co.uk>.

6 The Wolverhampton Episcopal Area comprises the archdeaconries of Walsall and Lichfield.

7 Due to an improvement in the diocese's finances, the last 3 of the planned 50 cuts did not in fact take place.

8 Bob Jackson was Archdeacon of Walsall and Bishop's Growth Officer within Wolverhampton Episcopal Area, from 2004 to 2009.

9 Bob Jackson, 'Going for Growth – April 2009 progress report' (unpublished).

10 Ad Clerum: A formal letter from the diocesan bishop to all clergy.